What Leading Voices Are Saying About Antoinette Tuff

"Not only did she make Michelle and me very proud, but she probably saved a lot of lives."

—President Barack Obama

"She is a reminder of what Christian courage looks like: She didn't need a weapon, just her faith and a willingness to love the unlovable and to share her own pain, failures, and struggles, knowing that the rest was in God's hands."

—Eric Metaxas, *BreakPoint*

"We should use her example to each our children's leaders—any of our leaders, really, and all of our children—the value of compassion and the power of empathy."

—*The Washington Post*

"She was a real hero in all of this. She just did a stellar job. She was cool, she was calm, very collected in all of this, maintained her wherewithal."

—*Fox News*

". . . an amazing illustration of calm and brinkmanship . . ."

—*The Guardian*

"The fascination at the heart of Tuff's tale, the reason it's riveting, is the way she used compassion and empathy to disarm a mentally ill man intent on killing."

—Salon.com

PREPARED
FOR A PURPOSE

C. 1

PREPARED
FOR A PURPOSE

The Inspiring True Story of How One Woman Saved
an Atlanta School Under Siege

ANTOINETTE TUFF
with Alex Tresniowski

BETHANYHOUSE
a division of Baker Publishing Group
Minneapolis, Minnesota

Published by Bethany House Publishers
11400 Hampshire Avenue South
Bloomington, Minnesota 55438
www.bethanyhouse.com

Bethany House Publishers is a division of
Baker Publishing Group, Grand Rapids, Michigan

Printed in the United States of America

Library of Congress Cataloging-in-Publication Data
Tuff, Antoinette.
    Prepared for a purpose : the inspiring true story of how one woman saved an Atlanta school under siege / Antoinette Tuff with Alex Tresniowski.
        pages cm
    Summary: "The true story of how one woman talked a school shooter down from the brink, and the amazing journey of how God prepared her for that moment"—Provided by publisher.
    ISBN 978-0-7642-1263-5 (cloth : alk. paper)
    1. Tuff, Antoinette. 2. School crisis management—Case studies. 3. School violence—Prevention—Case studies. 4. Women heroes—United States—Biography. 5. Heroes—United States—Biography. 6. African American women—United States—Biography. 7. African Americans—United States—Biography. 8. Christians—United States—Biography. 9. Atlanta (Ga.)—Biography. I. Tresniowski, Alex. II. Title.
    LB2866.5.T84 2014
    371.7'82—dc23   2013046918

Unless otherwise indicated, Scripture quotations are from the King James Version of the Bible.

Scripture quotations identified ESV are from The Holy Bible, English Standard Version® (ESV®), copyright © 2001 by Crossway, a publishing ministry of Good News Publishers. Used by permission. All rights reserved. ESV Text Edition: 2007

Scripture quotations identified NKJV are from the New King James Version. Copyright © 1982 by Thomas Nelson, Inc. Used by permission. All rights reserved.

Scripture quotations identified NLT are from the Holy Bible, New Living Translation, copyright © 1996, 2004, 2007 by Tyndale House Foundation. Used by permission of Tyndale House Publishers, Inc., Carol Stream, Illinois 60188. All rights reserved.

Scripture quotations identified RSV are from the Revised Standard Version of the Bible, copyright 1952 [2nd edition, 1971] by the Division of Christian Education of the National Council of the Churches of Christ in the United States of America. Used by permission. All rights reserved.

Cover design by Jennifer Parker with Paul Higdon
Cover photo of Antoinette Tuff by Mike Habermann Photography, LLC

Author is represented by Dupree/Miller & Associates

14   15   16   17   18   19   20   7   6   5   4   3   2   1

I dedicate this book to my best friend
and love of my new life—the almighty God.
Thank You for being there for me
and guiding me through all the pain,
and thank You for giving me two wonderful children
who have been the blessings of my life.

I also dedicate this book to my son,
Derrick.
You are a beautiful miracle,
and I am so proud God is using you to His glory.

//

God is our refuge and strength,
a very present help in trouble.
Therefore we will not fear,
even though the earth
be removed,
and though the mountains be
carried into the midst of the sea;
though its waters roar
and be troubled,
though the mountains
shake with its swelling.

Psalm 46:1–3 NKJV

//

Tuesday, August 20, 2013
Decatur, Georgia

Regular morning, I get up in darkness, 5:00 a.m., and I step softly so as not to wake my son. I turn on the lights in the kitchen and sit at the table and open my Bible, same as every morning. Before I do anything else I talk to God so I may know what to do with my day, how to act, what to say, who to help, and I start a new spiritual journey with the Lord—I *anchor* myself in the Lord. I do all this not knowing that in just a few hours a man will walk into my life and hold a fully-loaded AK-47 assault rifle to my head and say to me in a voice filled with pain and rage, "We are all going to die today."

This morning in the kitchen I begin with Psalm 23, the one I read every morning, the one everyone knows, the one that starts with "The Lord is my shepherd; I shall not want," and the one that says "though I walk through the valley of the shadow of death, I will fear no evil: for thou art with me." I read these words and fix them in my heart—again, not knowing that later this day a man will walk into the school where I work with enough bullets in his rifle and his backpack to kill more than half the children in the building, some as young as four years old, some as old as twelve, eight hundred and eighty children in all.

I fix breakfast for my own son, Derrick, his usual IHOP menu, because he doesn't like cold cereal, he likes a big hot breakfast, eggs and bacon and toast, and I wait for him to pull himself down the stairs with his arms, face first, feet dragging, because he cannot walk. And while he eats his hot breakfast I make him baked chicken with vegetables for lunch and a pork chop with potatoes for dinner and I put them in two separate bowls so he can take them out of the fridge and warm them up when he gets hungry later in the day, while I am still at work, at my third job.

And then I rush upstairs and shower and dress, and I sit with my son for a moment and let him know how much I love him. I get in my 2003 red GMC Envoy with 200,000 miles on it and I drive onto I-20 toward downtown Atlanta, and I get off at the Flat Shoals exit, and drive another three minutes until I am in the parking lot of the Ronald E. McNair Discovery Learning Academy on Second Avenue. I am at my desk by 7:00 a.m., on the nose, on a nice summer day, hot but pretty, and the kids are just now starting to walk in.

I do a morning's work, and the principal comes and asks me to sit in for the receptionist at the front desk at 12:30 p.m. when she goes to lunch. At 12:20 I am getting ready to relieve her when my phone rings.

That phone call is one of the most devastating calls in my life.

I am staggered by the news. I sit at my desk and cry like a child, and I think about how in just the last few months I nearly lost everything that mattered to me in this world. *Lord, what else will You put on my plate? You said You wouldn't put any more than*

10

I could handle, but now my plate is running over. No room even for gravy. So, Lord, what am I supposed to do now?

But I don't have time to wallow. It is 12:40 and I am late, so I pull myself together and I pack away my tears. I ask God to strengthen my heart, and He tells me to put aside my weight and do as He says, so I set aside my own problems and I sit at the front desk and I do my job.

FIVE MINUTES LATER THE UNTHINKABLE HAPPENS.

Five minutes later the unthinkable happens.

And when it happens my mind summons a passage in the Bible, John 10:10:

The thief cometh not, but for to steal, and to kill, and to destroy.

/////

That very morning a short, stocky twenty-year-old man gets up and dresses all in black. He lives in a bungalow on a wooded street in the Atlanta suburb of Decatur, and his neighbors know him to be quiet but polite, even friendly, and pretty much an average guy. Sometimes he takes care of some neighborhood children during the day.

The man zips open his black backpack and fills it with several boxes of bullets, until he can fit no more. He loads another magazine of bullets into an AK-47 assault rifle, a Russian-made weapon that was used in World War II and can shoot more than five hundred rounds of ammunition in less than a minute. It is one of the deadliest weapons in the world. The man steps out of his house on East Lilac Lane, gets in his car and goes down Camellia Drive to Second Avenue, until he arrives at the Ronald E. McNair Discovery Learning Academy. The school is less than a half mile from his house, so the drive is short. He pulls into the parking lot and finds an empty space near the front entrance, as close to the school as he can get.

He gets out and walks toward the front doors, his heavy backpack slung over his shoulder, his rifle pointed down by his side. The man waits for someone to be buzzed in, or walk out, then sneaks in through the open door. He walks three or four steps and turns right, into the very first room he sees—the front office. Now he is in a small, plain room, maybe ten feet by twelve feet, with windows facing the street that have their blinds pulled, and a door leading into a hallway that leads to the classrooms of the school, where hundreds of children are sitting at their desks or writing on chalkboards or coloring in books, innocent, unaware, in more danger than they could ever comprehend.

Because now this man is inside their school, in the front office, holding his weapon with both hands, waving it at the woman at the front desk—waving it at me.

"This is not a joke!" the man yells. "This is real!"

And then:

"*We are all going to die today!*"

And that is when I think of the passage in John 10:10, and I am gripped by a terror unlike anything I have ever known—ice cold, bone deep, bottomless, consuming, because I know I am in a room with a demon, and the demon has come to *steal, kill, destroy.*

The man dressed in black has only to shoot me and pass through the side door and encounter his first classroom full of children. All of that will take no more than three or four seconds of time, just the slightest tug on the trigger, the effort of a mere twenty steps, and then will come the nightmare, the hell, the recurring horror—Columbine, Virginia Tech, Sandy Hook—and McNair will become "McNair." I am so seized by fear I cannot think of a prayer to say, so I do what I do every day, I talk to my Father, and as I sit there, hands trembling, heart racing, rifle in my view, I ask one simple question:

> I AM GRIPPED BY A TERROR UNLIKE ANYTHING I HAVE EVER KNOWN.

"God, what are we going to do now?"

//////

My name is Antoinette Tuff—though my friends call me by my middle name, Marie—and before the events of August 20, 2013, there was nothing exceptional about my life, other than my faith in God. I was married for thirty-three years to the only man I ever knew or loved, and together we had two remarkable children, LaVita and Derrick. I've had my share of struggles, emotionally, spiritually, financially, and there were times I felt such misery and desperation I believed I could not bear them. Not all that long ago I tried to kill myself. I very nearly did.

GOD GUIDES US ALL ON
OUR JOURNEYS AND
PREPARES US FOR A
PURPOSE THAT IS NOT
ALWAYS OURS TO KNOW.

I was born into the Baptist faith and found my own way to God as I grew up. As an adult, God has been my constant companion, with me every step of the way, even when I couldn't feel Him, *most closely* at those times. He was there when my son was born with a serious neurological disorder, and when another disease took away his power to see and hear and walk. God was there in an Atlanta hospital in the summer of 2013 when my son fought his toughest battle, clinging to life by a fingertip. God was there when I got that devastating phone call in my office on August 20. God was with me when the gunman came in. And when the demon spoke of death, God spoke of life.

You may know some of the details of what transpired in the front office of McNair Academy on August 20. The events of that day made the newspapers and the nightly shows and the morning shows, too. But what happened in that room—what brought both the gunman and me to that place, at the same time on the same day—is not something that can be known from a police report, or a newspaper article, or a five-minute TV segment. Because what happened in that room is not about me, or even about the shooter—*it is about how God guides us all on our journeys and prepares us for a purpose that is not always ours to know.* "Trust in the Lord with all your heart, and lean not on your own understanding," it says in Proverbs 3:5–6. "In all your ways acknowledge Him, and He shall direct your paths" (NKJV).

The story you will read in this book, then—the story of what *really* happened in that room on August 20—is the story of a long and difficult journey that put me where I needed to be, when I needed to be there, and the many ways God prepared me for that day, just as He prepares us all for our true purpose on earth.

Just two weeks before I found myself across from that AK-47, I sat in a pew near the front of my church and listened as our pastor read in his soft voice from Hebrews 6. "When God made his promise to Abraham, since there was no one greater for Him to swear by, He swore by Himself, saying, 'I will surely bless you and give you many descendants,' says the Bible. And so after waiting patiently, Abraham received what was promised."

"You see," our pastor continued, "God's promise is to give us life, not death. He swore that to us with a solemn oath. And He made this promise because He wanted to give us *hope*. He wanted to give us the *encouragement* of hope. And that hope, it says in Hebrews, 'is an anchor for the soul, firm and secure.'"

I sat in church and let the words wash over me, and I thought, *Yes, that makes sense. Hope is an anchor.* I was going through so much hardship in my life, so much uncertainty and chaos, and sometimes I feel adrift in the world, so weak and inconsequential I might be swept away into oblivion at any moment. But no—my soul was not adrift. My soul was anchored to God by hope! What a beautiful, powerful realization that was. We must not allow the cares of our lives to dictate how we are going to act. We must let ourselves be anchored in God. And if we do, such faith will make us immovable.

I hope that as the story of my journey unfolds in these pages you will see something of your own journey in it, and come across words that speak to you, and maybe even help you feel the same anchoring power of hope and faith I felt on August 20. Because no matter where our lives take us—no matter what whirlwind journey we are on—we are all just waiting on the next assignment from God, hoping to be ordered by His steps and humbly asking the same, simple question of Him:

"God, what are we going to do now?"

///////////////////////////////////////

But evil does not spring
from the soil,
and trouble does not
sprout from the earth.
People are born for trouble
as readily as sparks
fly up from a fire.

Job 5:6–7 NLT

///////////////////////////////////////

CHAPTER ONE

TUESDAY, AUGUST 20, 2013

I got pretty good at making it look like I haven't been crying. I knew how to pull myself together pretty quick. None of my co-workers were aware of my divorce, because I kept all of those problems inside. So I knew how to act like nothing was wrong. Some deep breaths, some last sniffles, and I was okay. After the devastating call that came in on my cell phone, I heard my desk phone ring and I knew it was the receptionist, wondering where I was. I was already ten minutes late. I answered and told her I'd be there in a minute. I wiped away the evidence of how I felt and headed for the front office.

One of the young teachers at McNair, Belinda, stopped me just outside my office.

"Ms. Tuff, do you have a minute?" she said. "I could really use some help with my insurance forms."

"Sure," I said. "I've got to cover the front desk. Come with me."

In the front office the receptionist was talking with a parent. Belinda and I joined the conversation. Mostly it was idle chitchat. After a couple of minutes the receptionist left for lunch, and the parent said good-bye and left, too. The main door to the front office closed quietly behind her.

In that front room there's a desk for the receptionist, a counter, a few chairs, a sign-in sheet, and a monitor so you can see who's out front and buzz them through the main entrance, which is just a few steps from the office. It's a small and ordinary space that is the starting point to everywhere else in the school. Its whole purpose is for people to pass through on the way to where they're really going.

I got behind the desk and had Belinda spread out her papers, and we got to the matter of her insurance. That is one of my many jobs at McNair. My official title is bookkeeper, but really I do a lot more than pay the bills and keep the books. Anything that involves paperwork or forms usually ends up on my desk.

Belinda needed help understanding her benefits. She was a new teacher, and she had a new baby, and she only had thirty days to sign up for our insurance program, so she needed help enrolling. Belinda was a friend of mine, and in fact I'd helped her get hired at McNair. She sat behind the counter and I stood next to her, going over her papers. We talked a little about her baby boy. I helped her pick the right plan for her family. The front office seemed quiet. Everyone was somewhere else, having lunch.

Sometime around 12:45, just five or so minutes after I'd relieved the receptionist, the main door to the front office swung open.

I looked up and saw a man dressed completely in black. Black pants, black T-shirt, black shoes. I could tell he was young, and I could tell he was angry about something. His mouth was twisted into a frown and his brow was wrinkled up. He had short, cropped brown hair and his nose looked like it might have been broken at one time. In his hands he held a big, long black rifle—one hand on the barrel, the other on the trigger. The rifle was on a strap slung over his shoulder. I noticed it without any sense of alarm, because my first thought was, *Is this a joke? Some kid with a fake gun playing a prank? Or maybe a real gun, but he's just fooling around?* The danger of the situation didn't dawn on me right away. I guess my brain didn't want to process what I was actually seeing.

What changed all that were his eyes. They looked crazy. I don't know how else to put it. Eyes don't lie. If anyone had looked closely enough at my eyes that day, they'd have known I'd been crying. Now, the man's eyes were telling me the truth of what was happening. His eyes were wide open and burning with something. This man wasn't just serious, he was deadly serious. I felt that terrible squeezing in my stomach that terror brings. I knew before he said a word—I was in trouble.

"This is not a joke!" he yelled. "I need you to understand this is not a joke. I am here. This is real. We are all going to die today."

He was waving his gun at Belinda and me as he spoke, using it to demonstrate that he was in control. The gun was all he needed, but the yelling and the gesturing added to the terror. I snuck a quick look

> THIS MAN WASN'T JUST SERIOUS, HE WAS DEADLY SERIOUS.

21

at Belinda, and she turned and looked at me. I saw dread and panic on her face. I am sure she saw the same in mine. Neither of us dared speak. We turned back to the gunman, silent and in shock.

"Listen to me," he went on. "I need you to do exactly what I tell you. This is not a joke. This is serious." He took one step toward us and looked straight at Belinda. "You," he said. "Go tell everyone in the building I'm here. Tell them this is not a joke, this is for real."

Belinda looked at me as if to say, "Should I go?" She was worried about leaving me behind.

"Go ahead," I said aloud. "Do what he says. Go on, go."

I don't know why the gunman told Belinda to go and not me. I may never know that. I just know that he did.

Belinda paused for a moment, trying to steady herself. If she was as scared as I was, her legs must have felt like jelly. Then she turned on her heels and walked quickly out of the office, out a back door that leads to the teacher's lounge. It was lunchtime so there were plenty of teachers in there, and through the wall I could hear Belinda yell, "Intruder alert!" That is the phrase we're instructed to use to indicate a real security breach.

As soon as she said it I could hear chairs dragging against the tile floor and shoes scurrying and the whole commotion of a room emptying. I knew the gunman could hear it, too. I looked at him and saw the noise was making him even more agitated. He was pacing fast, like he couldn't control his energy, like he wanted to scream or bust out of his skin. Instead he raised his rifle to eye level and made a move for the side door.

The side door is the door that leads to the classrooms where the kids are.

"What are you doing?" I said. It was the first time I spoke directly to him.

"All this movement!" he said. "Tell them to stop moving!"

"They're just doing what you told them," I said. "Don't get alarmed."

But the gunman wasn't listening. The commotion was rattling him. He swung open the side door and aimed his rifle down the hallway. Just a few steps away there were two doors that led to the media center, where teachers and students were doing classwork, and further on down to the classrooms for second and third graders, and beyond that to the technology and music classrooms and the cafeteria. Probably two-hundred and fifty kids on this floor alone. In classrooms above and below our floor we had another six hundred or so children. If any of those kids were to wander into the hallway at that moment, they would be square in the gunman's sights.

Just past the gunman I saw a familiar face in the hallway—Russ, a staff member at McNair. Russ was scrambling and trying to duck into the media center, which was just outside the front office. He'd heard the cries of "intruder alert." Now he was running for safety.

The gunman spotted Russ and raised his rifle. He pointed it straight at him. Time seemed to stop. *He's going to kill Russ*, I thought. *Then he's going to kill the children.*

This was how it would begin.

/////

IF ANY OF THOSE KIDS
WERE TO WANDER INTO
THE HALLWAY AT THAT
MOMENT, THEY WOULD
BE SQUARE IN THE
GUNMAN'S SIGHTS.

God tells us to protect the children, the innocents among us, because children are God's special blessing to the world. "Take heed that ye despise not one of these little ones," it says in Matthew 18:10, "for I say unto you, that in heaven their angels do always behold the face of my Father." And for those who would bring harm to a child, "it is better for him that a millstone were hanged about his neck," Mark 9:42 tells us, "and he were cast into the sea."

But in today's world, not every child is spared harm, not every child is protected. We pack our children off to school in the mornings and try not to think of the terror and danger that could befall them. We try not to imagine the monster who would step out of the darkness, and in the clear light of day destroy the life of a child. But we know such monsters exist. We know dangers are everywhere. Sometimes children are on their own in this dangerous world. Sometimes it falls on them to protect themselves.

My father left my mother when I was two years old. I would not so much as lay eyes on him for the next eight years. I knew nothing about him—what he was like, why he left, where he went. All I knew was that every Christmas a package with my name on it would arrive in the mail, and I would open a present from my father, and I'd run to proudly show the doll or the toy or whatever it was to my mother, and she'd say, "Your daddy is always thinking about you. Your daddy loves you, you know."

Only many years later did I learn the truth of it. One Christmas a single package showed up addressed not only to me but also to my two older brothers, Timmy and John. Before then, each of us had always gotten our own package. This time there was only one. We opened it together and inside was a radio. It wasn't a good radio or a bad radio, it's just that it was a single radio, and not three individual gifts, one for each of us, like we expected.

"What are we supposed to do with this?" my brother Timmy asked my mother.

"Just enjoy it," she said.

I think it was John, two years older than me, who finally figured out that my father had not been sending us presents all along. In fact, it was our mother who sent them. Every year she'd buy three gifts, put them in separate boxes, take them to the post office, put our father's name in the return address, and mail them to our house in Alexandria, Virginia. If we'd known enough to look at the postmarks, we'd have seen the toys began and ended their journeys in the same place. But we didn't know enough. We were just happy to get presents from our long lost father. We were happy he was still thinking of us. Even when John confronted our mother about the deception, she refused to come clean.

"That's not for you to worry about," she said. "Your daddy loves you."

My mother never said a single cross word about the man who abandoned us all. Not a single complaint in all the years I've been alive. If my father harmed his children by walking out and disappearing from our lives, and surely he did, then it was my mother's mission to protect his image and soften the blow. I am sure she couldn't bear to tell us the truth—that our father didn't care a lick about us. But I also think she didn't want her children harboring ill will in their hearts. Maybe she understood that sometimes the real harm isn't the leaving but the anger left behind.

As a result of my mother's refusal to talk bad about my father, I didn't learn much about him at all. I still don't know how my parents met, or why they split apart. I don't know if they were happy for a few years, or always fighting. I don't know if they ever truly loved each other, though I like to believe they did. My mother still won't talk about those days. They are in the past for her, and that's where she wants to keep them.

In a way it didn't matter to me what my father was like, because I knew I got my personality from my mother. She was raised in High Point, North Carolina, a little southern town where the summers were long and hot and the grown-ups were strict but loving. She was proper in her behavior, and she taught her children manners and politeness and the fear of God, but at the same time she was tough and scrappy and unwilling to be bullied, and she wanted us to have that same toughness as we grew up. My mother was a survivor, and she raised three kids without any help from a man, and I felt proud that some of that spiritedness and sense of independence was passed along to me. As a kid I was feisty and outspoken, and I saw no reason to keep my opinions to myself. If I felt something needed to be said, I said it. I didn't like to be shushed or told what to do. Sometimes my mouth got me in trouble, but that was just the price of being me.

> SOMETIMES THE REAL HARM ISN'T THE LEAVING BUT THE ANGER LEFT BEHIND.

That is why, when my father suddenly came back into my life, things got out of hand.

When I was ten, my mother got sick. We didn't know what was wrong with her back then, but I later found out it was cancer. The sickness scared my mother pretty good, and she decided it was time we got to know our father, in case she died and we had to go live with him. That's why she got him to send us that radio as a Christmas present—she wanted to open the door that had long been shut between us.

The summer I turned ten, my mother sent my brothers and me to stay with my father and his new wife in their home in York, South Carolina. None of us were happy to go. I don't remember who drove us there, but I do remember the three of us standing on the front porch of the big, white colonial house and knocking timidly on the front door. The door opened and we saw two young girls, about my age, standing there. They looked at us for a few moments. Then they slammed the door in our faces.

Things only got worse from there.

That first summer in York—the summer I met my father— was long and hard and strange. It was obvious no one wanted us there—not my father's wife, not her five young daughters, and most certainly not my father. He made it clear we were just a giant imposition on him and his new family. Rather than have us sleep in the same bedrooms as his daughters, my father had Timmy, John, and me sleep on the living room floor. At chore time it seemed like me and my brothers always got more than our fair share handed to us. When vegetables needed picking in the garden outside, my father didn't send one of his stepdaughters, he sent me.

"I'm from the city," I told him. "We don't pick vegetables."

"Watch your mouth," he said back.

One day during that first summer I told my father I needed him to buy me something.

"I need feminine supplies," I said.

"Can't help you," my father said. He didn't say why.

"But I need them," I said. But there was no arguing with him. He wasn't denying me the supplies as any kind of punishment. He just didn't care enough to help me get them.

"You are treating that child mean," his mother—my grandma—warned him that day. "If you treat her bad you know she gonna be the one who buries you when you old." My father just grunted in response. And he kept being mean. It was as if Timmy, and John, and I were his stepchildren, and his wife's children were his real kids. And because they knew they came first, the girls were horrible to us—and particularly to me.

"You ain't ever gonna be anyone," one of them would tell me. "You're gonna be a bag lady."

"Yeah, you nobody," another would say. "You nothing and you always gonna be nothing."

Even my father's second wife had a habit of comparing me to her daughters, and not in a favorable way. According to her they were smarter than me, and prettier than me, and overall just better people than me. For sure they had more promising futures than me. I guess I half expected my father to occasionally stand up for me, but he never did. The dogging just went on.

The only saving grace that summer was the time I got to spend with my grandma, who owned the sprawling property that my aunt's house stood on, and the time I spent with my aunts—Aunt Bee, Aunt Katie, and Aunt Joann—who all seemed to like me a lot more than my daddy did. Grandma lived in a big house that was running distance from my aunt's place, and as soon as I learned I could go there, I went there pretty much every day. I didn't really know my grandma, and at first we didn't talk that much. But as the summer passed I think she came to like having me around. My brothers and I would help her feed her chickens and pigs, and we delighted in chasing her dirt-brown hogs around their pen and pulling on their tails so we could hear them squeal and then run away when they chased us. Sometimes we chased their babies around so the sows would get mad and come after us some more. We all thought that was the funniest thing in the world—running around screaming and laughing one step ahead of those angry hogs.

If we got to Grandma's early enough she'd cook us a good breakfast—bacon and homemade biscuits and sugary maple syrup. In the afternoons Grandma and I would go pick vegetables in her fifty-acre garden. It was so big we never made it all the way from one end to the other. Together we'd pick squash and tomatoes and blueberries, and take them back to the kitchen and cook them up and eat them on the spot. Those afternoons in the garden with my grandma were some of the best times of my whole childhood.

One day, as we were picking vegetables in a particularly dense part of the garden, I heard a hissing noise and looked down and saw a rattlesnake coming right at me. I dropped my vegetables and screamed out and started to run away, but Grandma grabbed me by the arm.

"No, baby, don't run away," she said. "You don't let the snake scare you. You scare the snake."

With that, Grandma stomped her feet and the rattlesnake slunk away. Then she casually went back to picking.

"**"DON'T EVER LET NOTHIN' SCARE YOU,"GRANDMA SAID.**

"Don't ever let nothin' scare you," she said as she pulled a fat, ripe tomato off a vine. "And don't you listen to what them kids tell you. They just bein' mean." I went back to picking, too, keeping one eye on the ground for snakes and repeating my grandma's words in my head, so I'd never forget them.

My mother battled her illness for three years, so for three summers we were sent back to live with our father. During the third summer, when I was thirteen, things really deteriorated. My father and I hadn't grown any closer in those three summers, only further apart, and as I got older our fights just got worse. I had an opinion on everything, and even though it was clear nobody cared what I thought, I voiced my opinions anyway. And while everyone felt they had the right to tell me what to do, I didn't listen to anyone and I only did what I wanted to do. That didn't sit too well with my father. But as far as I was concerned, who was he to have any authority over me at all? He didn't know what was best for me, because he wasn't really a part of my life. And anyway, he didn't care. So I wasn't about to let him boss me around.

One night my father told me to braid the hair of one of his wife's daughters. I was really good at braiding, and I did it for all my friends and a few of my cousins who lived nearby. But there was no way I was going to do it for one of his nasty stepkids.

"No," I said. "Let her braid it herself."

"You do as you're told," my father said, with more anger in his voice than I was used to.

"You do it if you want it done so much."

My father got out of his chair and walked to a closet. He pulled out a wooden broomstick and came to where I was standing. He pushed me to the floor and whacked me across the legs with the broomstick. I cried out in pain. He hit me again and again, some of the blows deflecting off my arms and my back as I tried to protect myself, some of them landing flush. I managed to scramble to my feet and I ran to the front door. I flung it open, but I was way too angry to leave without saying something. I don't think I've ever been angrier at anything than I was at that beating.

"I will never speak to you again!" I screamed at my father, who stood there holding the broomstick and breathing heavy. "I will spit on your grave!"

I slammed the door behind me and ran all the way to Aunt Bee's house and stayed with her and Grandma the rest of the summer. I didn't say another word to my father for the next six years.

When the summer ended I went back to Alexandria to be with my mother. But when I arrived I learned there was no home left to go to. My mother had lost our townhouse. She was physically better now, but the medical bills had been too much and she couldn't keep up with the rent. For the next year, my two brothers stayed behind in York and lived with my father.

As for my mother and me, for the next thirteen months we were homeless.

//////////////////////////////////////

THE SPIRIT HELPS US IN OUR
WEAKNESS; FOR WE DO NOT KNOW
HOW TO PRAY AS WE OUGHT, BUT THE
SPIRIT HIMSELF INTERCEDES FOR US
WITH SIGHS TOO DEEP FOR WORDS.

Romans 8:26 RSV

//////////////////////////////////////

CHAPTER TWO

TUESDAY, AUGUST 20, 2013

The gunman raised his rifle and pointed it at Russ. Russ was standing in the media room doorway, but I didn't know if he was going to make it inside. All it takes is one second for a man's life to be over. One squeeze of the trigger, and that's it.

I called out to the gunman again, trying to distract him.

"What are you doing?" I said loudly.

"Tell them to stop moving!"

"They're just doing what you said. Now come back in here. It's okay."

The gunman lowered his rifle, closed the door, and came back in the room. In the hallway I could hear the door to the media room slam shut. Russ was inside. He was safe, for now.

I don't know why the gunman didn't shoot Russ. I don't know why he came back when I told him to. Those aren't questions that occurred to me at the time. All I had back then was an understanding that the longer I kept the gunman in the front office, the longer it would be until he started shooting.

He went right back to pacing in the middle of the room. Suddenly the front office seemed very small. On an ordinary day you could pack a lot of teachers and parents and students in there, but on this day it felt like a closet. The gunman pacing back and forth made it seem even smaller. It was only the two of us in there, but I've never felt more suffocated.

"What is your name?" I asked.

He didn't answer. He just kept pacing.

"This is not a joke," he finally said. "I'm not playing. This is for real. We are going to die today."

He kept saying those words over and over. His anger was building, not subsiding. I just let him talk. The other understanding I had was that I shouldn't do anything that might agitate him further. I should do whatever I could to keep him calm. And though I didn't realize it at the time, looking back now I can see that I was doing something very specific in those early moments.

I was talking to the gunman like I would talk to any student.

I can't say I planned to do that. I didn't have time to plan anything. That was just the voice that I used—calm, assuring, authoritative. It just came out of me.

What the gunman couldn't see were my legs, which were trembling, or my hands, which were shaking. He couldn't hear my heart, which was beating two miles a minute. He could not see how utterly terrified I was. There is nothing as chilling as the realization that something horrible is happening. One moment ago it wasn't, and now it is. One moment ago your life wasn't anything you gave much thought to. Now your only thought is how your life could end at any second. I felt fear, real gut-level fear, which made every nerve in my body light up. But I also felt dread, a kind of soul-crushing dread, which made my body feel heavy and weak.

But along with all that I also felt immensely sad.

Very early on I realized I was in a room with death itself. I knew there was a chance, a very good chance, that I would never see Derrick and my daughter, LaVita, again. That I would never hug them or kiss them or tell them how much I love them again. I knew the man pacing before me was unstable in all his ways, and I knew the demon inside him was there to steal, kill, and destroy. I knew these things very well—I understood the gravity of my situation. I knew that every word out of my mouth could mean the difference between life and death—not just for me, but for everyone in the building. "Death and life are in the power of the tongue," it says in Proverbs 18:21. We must speak life into a situation, if we want God to be seen.

> I KNEW THAT EVERY WORD OUT OF MY MOUTH COULD MEAN THE DIFFERENCE BETWEEN LIFE AND DEATH.

So why, if I was so terrified, was I able to speak so calmly?

That very morning, in the kitchen of my home, I read Psalm 23—"The Lord is my shepherd . . . he leadeth me beside the still waters." I read the words, "I will fear no evil: for thou art with me; thy rod and thy staff they comfort me." And I read, "Thou preparest a table before me in the presence of mine enemies." The morning before that, at the same table, I read those very same words—"I will fear no evil: for thou art with me." And the morning before that, and the one before that, too. I read those words every morning, and in this way they seeped into my soul. So on August 20, when I asked God, "What are we going to do now?" I already had my answer. God was going to lead me beside the still waters. God was going to comfort me.

God was going to do the talking for me.

I did not have to pray to have this understanding—it was just there. In fact, I don't remember praying for help or comfort in those early moments, because those moments were just too chaotic. I only remember saying a single prayer the whole time, and not for anything you might think.

I prayed to God that He might hold my water.

You see, I had to go to the bathroom. I'd planned to go before I went to the front desk, but then that devastating phone call came, and then I was late, and now this was happening. I suddenly became aware I needed to go to the bathroom very, very badly. It was almost unbearable. I'm sure the terror gripping my body was making matters worse. So I prayed, "Lord, let me not have to go. Let my bladder be still." Like I said, not the prayer you might expect, but that was the prayer I thought to say. And for a moment at least, the unbearable urging went away. The fear and shaking and trembling stayed with me the whole time. But God held my water.

Other than that, I did not have to ask God for help. God gave me my calm, assuring tone because that's how He needed me to speak.

"What is your name?" I asked again, hoping to engage the gunman and get him to listen to me. So far he hadn't even made eye contact. When he barked his orders he looked past me, or at the ground, but never directly at me.

But he didn't answer. He just kept pacing and stressing how serious he was.

"I am not playing," he said. "I know I am going to die."

That's when the front door to the office opened and a middle-aged man walked in.

His name was Lou, and he was another staffer at the school. Lou was one of the happiest, most carefree souls you'd ever want to meet. He didn't walk places so much as glide there. He had a sparkle in his eyes and he was light on his feet. When he walked into the front office he was the same way—happy, carefree, maybe even whistling. I realized he hadn't heard about the Intruder Alert. He had no idea what was happening.

The gunman swung to face him and pointed the rifle toward him.

Lou looked up and noticed the gunman, and at first it didn't seem to faze him. He still had a big old smile on his face. Maybe, like me, his first thought was that this was a prank. He stopped in his tracks and the gunman shouted his same words.

"This is not a joke!" he said. "This is serious!" He jabbed his rifle toward Lou to make his point.

Lou froze. Before anything else could happen I spoke up. "Lou, come behind the counter with me," I said, motioning him toward me.

For some reason, Lou didn't hurry. He walked slowly, as if he *still* wasn't sure this was for real. There was no urgency in his movements, almost like he was sauntering. I wanted him to step on it so he'd be behind the counter and less exposed—and also so the gunman wouldn't get angrier.

But it was too late for that.

Before Lou could make it behind the counter, the gunman took his AK-47 and fired. The sound was deafening. The shooting had begun.

/////

When you are young and your momma is Baptist, you spend a lot of time at church. Momma took us to church all the time, and it seemed there was always something going on there. There was morning service and evening service and chicken dinners and vacation Bible school and activities and events and get-togethers and choir practice and Sunday school. Basically your church was your home away from home. I didn't mind going, and most of the time I liked it fine, but I can't say I took to it with any kind of fervor. Not like my older brother Timmy, anyway.

> BEFORE LOU COULD MAKE IT BEHIND THE COUNTER, THE GUNMAN TOOK HIS AK-47 AND FIRED.

Timmy was *really* into God. As a kid I was too busy playing with my friends to put too much thought into the words of the Bible, but Timmy read them closely, and what's more, he *acted* on what he read. One year, when he was a teenager, he even went on a forty-day fast, just like Jesus in the wilderness.

My other brother John and I couldn't quite understand why he was doing it, but our skepticism didn't bother him in the least. He'd just say to us, "Y'all going to hell."

The church never stopped being our home away from home, and for a long while it was our only home.

After I told my father I would spit on his grave and I came back to be with Momma, she and I embarked on a long journey with only the mercy of God to guide us. After losing her rented townhouse apartment, Momma had put her belongings in storage, and she and I moved in with her friend Connie. Connie had a three-bedroom apartment in northeast Washington DC. She lived with her daughter, Cheralyn, and her twin sons, Melvin and Kelvin, who were about my age. We stayed there for a couple of months before moving on to another friend's home for a spell. Then we moved again, and again.

In just a little over one year Momma and I moved fourteen times, sometimes staying with friends, sometimes with strangers who were fellow churchgoers. Sometimes I had my own bed, but most of the time I slept on sofas and floors. Everywhere we went we outstayed our welcome, so it seemed we were always packing up and moving on. That is what it means to be homeless. We weren't on the street, but we didn't have a roof to call our own, either.

Sometimes it was me who got us kicked out of a place. I told you I had a sassy mouth, and I pretty much said whatever was on my mind. Well, not everyone appreciated my honesty, or my unwillingness to be bossed around. "You done it again," Momma would tell me. "Time for us to go." So it was off to yet another place we weren't wanted.

Things never got any better for me than they were at Connie's house. Connie cooked the most delicious chicken liver dinners, and I got along really well with her kids. In particular I had a crush on her son Melvin. At the same time I was also interested in a boy I knew from the neighborhood named Tony. Tony was my first real love—well, puppy love, anyway. So I had Tony, and I had Melvin, and I had no time at all for this other boy who always came by to have dinner at Connie's and took to staring at me a lot and liked to tease me and follow me around, and who one day sat at Connie's kitchen table with me and started crying and saying over and over, "Antoinette, I love you and I want to be with you."

His name was Terry, and he was friends with Melvin and Kelvin. When I met him he was seventeen, four years older than me. He had a sweet, sunny smile and a way of paying attention to you like he was really listening to what you had to say. Early on I pretty much ignored him, but that didn't slow him down. He came to dinner most every night, and he hung around afterward, never straying far from my side. Some days I'd have to take our clothes to a nearby Laundromat and Terry would show up and walk me there, and wait to walk me back home. Other days he came by Connie's and asked me to come with him to play ball or just hang out.

"Wanna go to the movies?" he asked me one day. I got a little money from Momma, and we went to the movies, just the two of us.

"Wanna go to McDonalds?" he asked another day. So we'd go to McDonalds and share a single meal because neither of us had enough money for two.

WE WERE ALWAYS
PACKING UP AND
MOVING ON. THAT IS
WHAT IT MEANS TO BE
HOMELESS. WE WEREN'T
ON THE STREET, BUT WE
DIDN'T HAVE A ROOF TO
CALL OUR OWN, EITHER.

Before we were homeless Momma enrolled me in a mixed-culture grade school in Virginia. But once we were at Connie's, my mother put me in an all-black school for the first time in my life. It was a rough place, and there were a lot of fights. To be honest, I was scared most days I was there. I told this to Terry, and he began walking me to school in the mornings and showing up to walk me back home in the afternoon. Sometimes he hung around the school playground all day shooting hoops, just waiting for me. I can't say Terry saved me from every fight—I had my share of brawls with other students—but he surely saved me from some.

For a while I continued to go on dates with Tony even while Terry was fawning all over me. The truth is, I did not fall in love with Terry from the start. If anything, I was in love with Tony. And that fact drove Terry crazy. Sometimes he would even cry when I told him I was going to see Tony.

"Don't you understand I love you?" he'd say.

It felt bad to see him cry, but that didn't stop me from seeing Tony.

Even after Momma and I had to leave Connie's—I don't remember why, probably something I said—Terry kept showing up to whatever new apartment we moved into. He was always around, waiting for me. He paid so much attention to me that over time I got used to having him in my life. My father wasn't there, and neither were my brothers, and it was Terry who filled that void. My life was so uncertain and unstable, but Terry was a constant. I came to really like him, and to rely on him, and before too long I forgot all about Tony and Melvin.

Then one day, when I was in a department store with a couple of friends, I passed by a bridal shop. Somehow I convinced the clerk to let me put on one of the wedding gowns, and I had my friend take a picture of me in it. Then I sent the photo to Terry with the words "What do you think?" written beneath it.

I guess it was right around that time I realized I was in love with Terry, and that I expected to spend the rest of my life with him.

/////

In the seventh grade, I dropped out of school because Momma and I were moving so much. Bouncing from place to place fourteen times in one year makes it kind of hard to keep up with your homework. Terry had dropped out of school too, and when he was nineteen he joined Job Corps, a government-run program that provides free schooling and vocational training to kids sixteen and older. It's similar to a regular school, in that you stay on campus and you go to classes and you wind up with a GED or a trade. Terry went to an all-boys Job Corps program in Harpers Ferry, West Virginia, and when he left I missed him. Sometimes I'd go see Terry in West Virginia on visitor's day. And once a month he would come back home and look for me and spend time with me no matter where I was living. Then he'd go back and we would write letters to each other every day. I kept these letters for years and years afterward.

So, when I turned sixteen, I signed up with the Job Corps in Charleston, West Virginia, just so I could be closer to Terry. Within a few months he transferred from Harpers Ferry to Charleston, so he could be closer to me.

After that, we were almost never apart.

We both left Job Corps after two years, me with new typing and administrative skills and Terry with welding and construction skills. By then my mother was renting an apartment in DC, and I asked if I could move in with her.

She flat-out told me no.

"It's your mouth got us kicked out of all them other places," she explained.

Terry asked his mother if we could stay with her in her DC apartment, and she said no, too. All of a sudden, I was homeless again. Terry and I wound up sleeping on the ground floor of the apartment building where his mother lived, in the dark space beneath the stairwell. We used our little bags of clothing as pillows and we snuggled up to each other and slept as best we could, down there with the dust and the dirt and the mice, and the next day, when Terry's mother went to work as a nurse at a hospital, we'd use her apartment to shower and eat and maybe even sleep a little in his bed there. She didn't mind us using her apartment when she wasn't there. But because we weren't married she refused to let us sleep there together at night.

I can't even say I was miserable sleeping under a stairwell, because I had Terry, and back then that was all I thought I needed. He was really very sweet to me, always looking out for me and taking care of me and making sure I was as safe as could be. He went to work as a driver every day and he brought back food and clothes and whatever we needed. Meanwhile I was working as a baker in a local Au Bon Pain, so I was bringing home a little money, too. Despite the fact that we were squatting illegally beneath a stairwell, it seemed to me that Terry and I were pretty much like any other young couple in love.

The pattern of me bouncing from place to place was not broken once I left Momma. It just continued with Terry. A friend of his knew someone who managed a residential property in southeast Washington DC, and Terry arranged for us to sleep in a vacant apartment there. We'd show up late at night, sleep on the bare wooden floor, and sneak out early in the morning. Once again, that didn't seem like such a terrible arrangement to me; on the contrary, I was happy to be able to sleep in a place with walls and a door. After the apartment got rented we stayed with one of Terry's friends for a few weeks, and then with his ex-girlfriend, which wasn't ideal because she kept walking around in sexy lingerie trying to win him back.

> I CAN'T EVEN SAY I WAS MISERABLE SLEEPING UNDER A STAIRWELL, BECAUSE I HAD TERRY.

You might think the last thing I would want to do in a situation like that—no home, not much money, uncertain future—was to add a baby to the mix.

But remember, I was only nineteen, and the one thing I wanted more than anything else in the world—a happy family of my own—wasn't something I was interested in waiting too long to make happen. So right in the middle of all that turmoil Terry and I decided to have a child and I got pregnant. It was not an accident—it was very planned. Terry and I talked a lot about it and we knew we wanted to be with each other forever and have a big family and all that, and we figured we'd find a way to make it work. We even entered into a pact, in which we both promised never to have children with anyone else but each other. Even if for some unlikely reason we split up, the pact would hold—no kids unless they were his and mine together.

That's not to say I wasn't scared to death when I went to a prenatal clinic in DC and a nurse told me I was pregnant. The first words out of my mouth were, "No way, I can't be pregnant." As much as I wanted a child, I was still shocked to hear I was having one. But Terry wasn't, and he calmed me down and assured me everything would be just fine. Terry was my hero in those days, going with me to prenatal classes, rocking me to sleep at night, letting me lay across his body like he was a big pillow, rubbing my belly and talking and singing to our unborn child.

During my pregnancy, Terry and I moved into a room in a run-down boarding house in the roughest section of southeast DC. From the outside the place looked like it should be condemned, and on the inside it was even worse. It was only two floors, with three or four bedrooms upstairs and two downstairs, one of which was ours. The other belonged to a creepy older man who ran a whorehouse out of his room. Every night strange men would bang on the door and greet loud and painted women and disappear inside, and in my room I would have to bury my head in a pillow so I wouldn't hear the awful noises coming through the walls.

One night, as I was coming into the boarding house, the creepy older man stopped me in the hallway and offered me a hundred dollars for oral sex. I was twenty and seven months pregnant, but he didn't seem to mind. I brushed past him, but he followed me down the hallway and kept asking me to have sex, so I ran into the kitchen and grabbed a knife and I chased him back down the hallway screaming, "If you ever come near me again I will kill you. Don't you *ever* talk to me like that again."

When I told Terry about it, he called his mother and begged her to let us move in with her. Once again, she said no. I called my mother, too, and asked her if we could stay with her. And she, too, said no. So we were stuck living next to a whorehouse, me, Terry, and our soon-to-be baby child.

Finally, when I only had a few weeks to go, my mother agreed to let me move in with her in her apartment in Temple Hills, Maryland, across the Anacostia River from DC. She was able to get some of my food stamps because we were there, so that probably weighed in her decision. Terry went to stay with his mother, and some nights I stayed with him there, and other nights I stayed with my mother. I was in my mother's apartment when my water broke.

Momma rushed me to the hospital and from there called Terry, who was back in DC, to let him know it was happening. Terry insisted my mother hand the phone to me, because he had something to tell me.

"I'm on my way," he said. "Don't have the baby till I get there! Whatever you do, wait till I get there!"

Terry ran all the way from southeast DC to the hospital in Maryland—a good ten miles if it was anything. We didn't have a car back then, so Terry ran everywhere all the time. When he burst into my hospital room he was sweating like a horse and so dehydrated somebody had to give him juice to drink or else he would have passed out. Luckily for him, but not for me, my labor lasted thirteen hours. I was scared before Terry got there, but once he was by my side I was okay. I was ready to have our baby. I was ready to have my family.

LaVita was late in coming; she was supposed to show up in March, but I finally had her—a beautiful, healthy little girl—on April 15. The nurse gave her to me first, and I held her and kissed her tiny forehead, and then I handed her to Terry. As soon as he took LaVita in his arms, he got all emotional. And because he'd spent so much time talking and singing and praying over our daughter in my belly, it seemed to me like she was instantly in heaven in his arms. She was going to be a daddy's girl, I could tell that right from the start.

Terry and I finally had the family we wanted. And just a few weeks after LaVita was born, Terry got down on one knee and handed me a small engagement ring he bought with money from his driving job, and asked me to marry him.

I said yes.

The ring was too big for my finger and I asked Terry to take it back to the jewelry store to get it sized, but he was always too busy and for months he never did. I still wore it, but I had to be extra careful not to let it fly off my finger. Finally, out of the blue one day, Terry asked me for the ring and told me he was going to get it sized. A week passed, and then another, and then a whole month, and then two. Every few days I'd ask Terry about the ring and he'd say they were still working on it, or he was too busy to go get it, or some other excuse. I bit my tongue, but I kept hounding him to get my ring back.

We were living with Terry's mother by then, and one day I decided to go to service at his family's church, rather than with my mother. It was the first time I had ever set foot in his family's church. I walked in holding baby La Vita, and right away I noticed people in the congregation looking at me funny. I didn't know why and I didn't let it bother me. I kept going to worship there, and I even joined the choir.

And it was on the platform one Sunday, while I was singing with the choir during morning service, that I looked over at one of the other choir members, a girl about my age, and I saw that she was wearing an engagement ring.

My engagement ring.

Terry had proposed to her, too. He was engaged to both of us.

//////////////////////////////////////

FOR WE WRESTLE NOT AGAINST
FLESH AND BLOOD, BUT AGAINST
PRINCIPALITIES, AGAINST POWERS,
AGAINST THE RULERS OF THE
DARKNESS OF THIS WORLD.

Ephesians 6:12

//////////////////////////////////////

CHAPTER THREE

TUESDAY, AUGUST 20, 2013

For a moment I thought the gunman had fired at us, and I waited to see Lou crumple to the ground, or maybe it would be me. But neither of us fell. The gunman had aimed two feet right of us, and down at the floor, and fired one shot.

The gunshot was incredibly loud, and then I heard the bullet bounce off the floor and ricochet across the room. I didn't know that bullets ricochet. But I heard this bullet whiz in the air and hit another wall, and I heard the shell casing come to rest on the counter to my left. All that happened in a split second. The harsh smell of a spark of fire filled the air.

I turned to Lou and saw he was clutching his chest. He looked like he was having a heart attack. It wouldn't have surprised me if he was. The sound of the gunshot took the level of terror in the room to a whole new level. This man not only had a deadly weapon but he was more than willing to use it. I felt my own heart seize in my chest, like someone had grabbed it and wouldn't stop squeezing. A cold, heavy reality occurred to me again—I could die at any moment.

Now Lou was bracing himself against the desk, still holding his chest. I couldn't tell if he was having a heart attack or not, and I don't think Lou could either.

"You," the gunman said, pointing his rifle at Lou. "Leave now and tell everyone this is happening."

Lou looked at me. All the cheerfulness was gone now. His look was the same one my friend Belinda gave me—the one that said, "Is it okay to leave you here?"

"Go!" the gunman repeated. "Go now!"

Lou looked at me one last time.

"Do what he says," I told him. "Go."

Lou walked to the back door and hustled out of the room. *Now* he was moving fast. The door closed behind him, and once again it was just the gunman and me. The gunman started pacing again. I sat shaking in my chair. My hands were shaking so hard I couldn't have held a pencil if I tried. The gunshot changed everything. If I had any doubts about what the gunman had in mind, they were gone now. But at least no one had been killed yet.

The gunman stopped pacing and turned toward me, still looking down and avoiding eye contact.

"Get on the intercom and tell everyone what is going on," he said. "Let them know I am here and what is going on."

I took hold of the intercom microphone and switched it on. It shook in my hand and I tried to keep it steady.

"We have an intruder in the building," I managed to say in a calm and measured tone, and I could hear my own voice echoing over the speakers in the nearby rooms. "This is not a drill, this is real. Follow the procedures of an intruder alert. Everybody stay calm, and everything is going to be all right. We have an intruder in the building."

I put the microphone down, and the gunman seemed satisfied with my announcement. I was just happy that now everyone in the school knew they were in danger. Hopefully the teachers would start getting the children out of the school somehow. The longer the gunman stayed with me, the more time they would have.

"Now call 9-1-1," the gunman ordered. "Call 9-1-1 and call a news station. Tell them I'm going to start shooting."

I picked up the phone and punched in 9-1-1 and waited for an operator. Within seconds a woman came on the line.

"What is your emergency?"

"Yes, ma'am, I'm on Second Avenue in the school, and he says he's going to start shooting," I said.

"Okay, hold on," the dispatcher said.

"Do not let anybody in the building, including the police," I said, and then, more forcefully, *"Do not let anybody in the building, including the police."*

> THE GUNSHOT CHANGED EVERYTHING. IF I HAD ANY DOUBTS ABOUT WHAT THE GUNMAN HAD IN MIND, THEY WERE GONE NOW.

"Stay on the line with me, ma'am," the dispatcher said. "Where are you?"

"I'm in the front office."

Before I could say anything else I saw the gunman take one of the plastic chairs in the office, open the front door, and use the chair to prop the door open. Then he walked the few steps to the main entrance of the school. From my desk I could see him push open one of the front glass doors. Then I saw him raise his rifle and point it outside.

Then he started shooting.

One shot, then another, then more. *Pop, pop, pop, pop.* Loud as anything you'll ever hear. It was like some kind of war movie. I felt like I couldn't breathe.

"Oh," I said into the phone, "he just went outside and started shooting."

And then, as if asking permission, I said, "Can I run?"

"Can you get somewhere safe?" the dispatcher asked.

I asked her again if I should go, or should I just stay because the gunman was going to see me go down the hallway and maybe start shooting. Instinctively I got up on my feet. Just a few yards away the gunman was still shooting. I kept my eyes on him. This was my chance to run out the back door, hopefully before he noticed and turned his rifle on me. I tried to move my feet but nothing happened. I tried again and still they didn't move. It was now or never. If I didn't run now I might not get another chance.

The gunman stopped shooting, walked back into the front office, and slammed the door behind him, huffing and puffing.

I was still there, behind my desk. Turns out I wasn't supposed to run.

//////

I suppose when I found out Terry had used my engagement ring to propose to another woman I could have left him on the spot and never looked back. But I didn't. Because the truth is, I loved Terry more than I loved myself, and more, even, than I loved God. I couldn't understand how that was possible, but it was. So I forgave Terry and I stayed with him.

Turns out I wasn't supposed to run then, either.

It's not like I took the news well. I felt the hard slap of betrayal across my face. I felt the ugly lowness that comes with being disregarded. I was only beginning to recognize the wound my father caused by walking out on me, and now here was Terry looking like he might do the same. The sight of my ring on that woman's finger pushed every other thing out of my head, so all I could do was dwell on the hurt and anguish I felt. And I felt something else—anger. I felt more anger toward Terry than I had toward anyone since my daddy beat me with a broomstick.

In our early years together, Terry had strayed more than once, but we were younger back then and I knew he would always come back to me in the end. And he always did. But now things were different. We had a daughter now. Not only that, he'd cheated on me right out in the open. Everyone knew about it except me. He'd made a fool of me in front of the whole church. I deserved more respect than that. And I was going to get it.

"No more," I told Terry when I finally got him alone. "Enough is enough. Either we're getting married, or it's over."

Terry did what he always did—he chose me. You see, I believed in Terry, and I believed in us—and even if Terry didn't yet, my belief was strong enough for both of us. With my whole being

I believed Terry was a good man who would always do right by me, despite stumbling every now and then. It never occurred to me to run away from Terry. By his side was the only place in the world I wanted to be.

Terry cut it off with the girl in the choir, but when he said something about getting the ring back, I told him I never wanted to see it again, she could keep it. Instead we went to the jewelry store and bought two new rings, one for each of us. Expensive rings, too. We bought them with only a little cash down, and we paid for those rings for many, many years. But I believed it was worthwhile. I only planned on getting married once. I was twenty-three and I'd known Terry for ten years now. I was absolutely sure all his foolishness was behind him.

Even so, the church coordinator for our wedding refused to marry us because she said Terry didn't really love me and wasn't serious about the marriage. I thought she was dead wrong, and I told her so. Not long after that a woman came up to me on the street and told me I shouldn't get married because the man I was planning to marry was no good. Well, I had no idea who she was, and I didn't pay any attention to her, either. Looking back, I can see why she said what she said, and why the church coordinator did what she did. Like my grandmother always told us, grownups have a lot more wisdom than we children. And maybe that woman on the street was an angel sent by God, trying to steer me on a different path. Were these bad omens I should have paid attention to? Terry giving my ring to another woman? Our church coordinator refusing to marry us? A stranger telling me he was no good? Maybe they were, and maybe I should have paid attention. But I didn't. Like I said, I loved Terry more than I loved myself.

Terry and I waited until we got an income tax refund check, and we used that money to throw a modest wedding. Terry's mother's friends cooked all the food—Jamaican chicken, curried dishes, even some Chinese food—and we held the ceremony in the backyard of one of his mother's best friends in Maryland. Someone decorated the yard with a little archway and flowers, and we set up a hundred white folding chairs.

One of those chairs—as unlikely as it may sound—was for my father.

I hadn't seen my father since he whipped me ten years earlier. But in my mind, despite everything he'd done to me, despite not being there for me, I always thought of having him walk me down the aisle when I got married. I wanted a traditional wedding, and that was the traditional thing to do. So I got up my nerve and I called him a few weeks before the wedding.

"I'm getting married," I told him, "and I want you to walk me down the aisle."

He was silent for a moment. Then he said, "Okay, I would be happy to." I could tell by his voice that he meant it—he was happy I had asked.

LaVita, who was three by then, was our flower girl. She wore the most precious little lavender dress and a ribbon in her hair. Terry wore a lavender and white tuxedo to match. Terry's mother offered to pay for a wedding dress and she even took me shopping for it, and the one we picked was beautiful—smoother and silkier than anything I'd ever touched. I also had a white pillbox hat and a custom-made veil.

When the time came, LaVita walked down the aisle tossing rose petals and crying the whole way. She only stopped after her daddy scooped her up by the altar, daddy's girl that she was. Then it was my turn. I walked down the aisle, my father holding my arm, to a romantic Luther Vandross song. The Reverend Harper, my pastor at the Mentrotone Baptist Church on B Street in DC, officiated. Terry's uncle, Apostle Tuff, said a prayer over our wedding. We exchanged our vows.

On a warm and sunny August day Terry and I became man and wife.

A friend of Terry's mother worked for the local paper, so the next day a photo from the wedding ran on the front page. It showed Terry and me holding each other and laughing in the sunlight. We looked like the two happiest people in the world.

On that day I believe we were.

Terry went to work driving trucks for a shipping company, and I found a job doing administrative work for a government agency in Virginia. We rented an apartment in the Murraygate complex in Alexandria, and we started our lives as a family. Within a couple of years of our wedding we decided to have another child. Terry really wanted a son, and he told me if I had another girl we'd have to keep having babies until we had a boy, even if we wound up with enough kids to start our own baseball team. I told him he'd better rub my belly and pray hard because this was the last baby I was planning on having.

His prayers must have worked, because the sonogram showed we were having a son. We chose the name Derrick.

Terry was with me at Alexandria Hospital in Virginia when I went into labor. It was a short labor, only two hours. When the baby arrived, the first thing I noticed was that his head was tilting way over to one side. It looked unnatural. When a nurse put him in my arms I tried to straighten his head, but it just fell right back to the side. The doctor came over and looked the baby over and said a word I'd never heard in my life.

"He has torticollis," the doctor said.

Even before I knew what that meant I felt like I might scream out in defiance. It was a medical word, and in the moments after your child is born, you don't want to hear any medical words, only words like, "What a beautiful, healthy baby you have there." I felt like I wanted to scream at the doctor, "No, no he doesn't. He doesn't have anything like that. Stop talking and let me and my baby be."

I would soon learn torticollis is an abnormality that affects the neck muscles and results in a child's head leaning out of position, either to the side, forward, or backward. It can be caused by things like muscular fibrosis or congenital spine abnormalities, or by some kind of injury. It didn't matter to me how my son got it. All I wanted to know was if it could be fixed.

The hospital got us a physical therapist who worked with Derrick in his first few months. His neck got a little stronger, but his head still wasn't right. Every time I looked at him I felt my joy

IN THE MOMENTS
AFTER YOUR CHILD
IS BORN, YOU DON'T
WANT TO HEAR ANY
MEDICAL WORDS.

being dragged down by dread—the dread of not knowing what would happen. But I also told myself it could be worse. Aside from the torticollis, Derrick was a happy, playful, beautiful little boy. He was curious and bubbly and just really cheerful. I knew he was a blessing the moment I saw him, and I never stopped believing that. I just wanted so desperately for him to be healthy.

At six months I started taking Derrick to a special school where he got more physical therapy. A few months after that, when he started trying to talk, we noticed his speech was slurred. He was trying to say certain words but they weren't coming out right. So we brought in a speech therapist to go with his physical therapist. It was a lot for a little boy to handle, but Derrick handled it great. He never lost his joyous spirit. Meanwhile, I just kept praying.

When Derrick turned one he still hadn't started walking, and I prayed he was just a late starter. But when he finally began rising up on his little feet and trying to move forward, he had a lot of trouble. It was like his legs were too weak to support him. As the weeks went on, it only got harder for him to walk. Other kids his age were racing around, but Derrick couldn't walk five paces without stumbling.

That's when I was struck by a terrible truth—something is really wrong with my boy.

Still, no one who ever examined him told me he had any serious problem. We all just kept working with him and praying he would get better. Though he wasn't walking normally, Derrick found a way to dash around like any other kid—not running, exactly, but sort of like running—and it was heartening to see him try to keep up with his little friends.

Then, one day when he was two, Derrick was scrambling around our living room chasing after his big sister. In one corner of the living room I had a table that displayed all the crystal plates and glasses we'd received as wedding gifts. All of a sudden Derrick took off toward the table and didn't stop. He crashed right into it and fell to the ground and the crystal landed on top of him and shattered all around him. I rushed over and picked him up in my arms, looking for blood. But there wasn't a scratch on him. In fact, he wasn't hurt at all. When I put him down he just kept dashing around, as if nothing had happened.

But something had happened. Derrick hadn't *seen* the table.

There was something wrong with his eyes, too.

We brought in an occupational therapist—Derrick's third kind of therapist—who taught him how to do things he was having trouble doing. He had almost no peripheral vision at all, and to him things that were close looked like they were five hundred feet away. Meanwhile he was having more and more trouble walking, and his speech was getting worse. It was like his body was deteriorating, and we had no idea why.

From kindergarten through the third grade, Derrick managed to get around on his own, hard as that was. But by the fourth grade his legs were so weak we had to get him a small walker. He didn't let the walker slow him down; if anything it made him quicker. Yet his legs continued to weaken, and as his upper body grew it became too heavy for his legs to support.

By the sixth grade Derrick needed a wheelchair.

Things got even worse from there. Derrick started acting out at school, and he was diagnosed with attention deficit hyperactivity disorder—as if he didn't already have enough disorders. Then one day I noticed he was struggling to pick something up. I looked at his hands and saw his fingers were starting to curl. *Dear God,* I thought, *what now?*

So many things were wrong with Derrick, and yet no one was able to tell us what was causing it all. For a while I was happy no doctor could diagnose him. I was terrified of losing him, and I figured no news was good news. Whatever else went wrong, we would handle it. But what I couldn't handle was a diagnosis that took my child away.

When Derrick was getting ready to enter the seventh grade, a doctor performed a general biopsy and had us come to his office to discuss the results.

"Your son has something called Charcot-Marie-Tooth disease," he told us quietly.

I'd never heard of any such thing, and I wondered what his teeth had to do with it. But Tooth is actually the last name of one of the three doctors who discovered the disease. CMT is an inherited neurological disorder that affects the peripheral nerves that connect to the body's muscles and sensory organs. The disease causes weakness in the legs and feet and the loss of muscle mass in the lower limbs. Sooner or later it attacks your hands, too.

There is no known cause, and no known cure. If you have it, you have it for life.

To hear my boy had this disease was as painful as anything I'd ever felt. I guess not having a name for what was wrong allowed me to hold onto some kind of hope, but now I knew my son would likely never get better. He was not only disabled, he had more than one disability, and he would always struggle to do simple things other people did without thinking. The thought of how much pain and suffering my son would have to go through was almost too much for me to bear. I tried to be strong, and I tried not to be angry at God. I prayed for the wisdom and forti- tude to handle what we'd been given. But the truth is, it was hard. Those times were very trying times. If I could have absorbed all the problems my son had to deal with, I would have done it in a heartbeat. But I couldn't. I couldn't make his suffering go away.

It then fell to me to be strong so Derrick wouldn't see how devastated I was, and most of the time I succeeded.

But not all the time.

There were many days when I'd watch Derrick hobble around, or see him stare at the sky with his broken eyes, or drop a pencil he couldn't hold onto, and I'd be powerless to stop my tears. I'd burst out crying right in front of him, and I'd try desperately to muffle the sound. I did not want him to feel the sorrow I felt. But despite everything that is wrong with my son, there is nothing wrong with his mind. He is a bright and clear thinker, and he is more sensitive and soulful and thoughtful than most. He writes music and songs and he sings those songs to help me feel better along the way. He always seemed to know just when I was sad, and he always knew why I was sad, too.

So my boy would push himself over to me in his walker or his wheelchair, and he would take my hand in his small, closing hand, and he would whisper these sweet words to me.

I TRIED TO BE STRONG,
AND I TRIED NOT
TO BE ANGRY AT
GOD. I PRAYED FOR
THE WISDOM AND
FORTITUDE TO HANDLE
WHAT WE'D BEEN
GIVEN. BUT THE TRUTH
IS, IT WAS HARD.

"Mommy," he would say, "it's okay. If you see me cry, *then* you can cry. But I'm not crying, because I know God is going to heal me. So you can hold on to my faith today."

You see, Derrick believed in himself, and in God, enough for both of us.

////

The gunman came back into the front office, his rifle still smoking. He was breathing hard and his face was a mask of rage and confusion. He was losing control of himself. *He has sprayed his gun outside,* I thought as he barreled back toward me. *Now he will spray inside. He is going to kill the children.*

I spoke to him calmly, in the same voice I'd used before.

"She's getting the police," I said, holding the phone in my hand. "She's telling them to back off for you, okay?" I said this as if he hadn't just fired off his AK-47.

"Tell them to stop moving now!" he yelled out.

"Okay, stop all movement on the ground," I told the dispatcher. "Stop all movement on the ground."

"Tell them, don't use the police radio or school radio unless it's an emergency," he said.

I repeated his words.

"Are you talking to the shooter?" the dispatcher asked.

"Yes, that's what he's telling me to tell them," I said. Then I addressed the gunman.

"What did you want me to tell her, sir?"

"Hang up the phone!" he yelled. "*Hang up now!*"

I lowered the phone and put it in its cradle—but before I did I pressed the hold button. The call was not disconnected. The 9-1-1 dispatcher was still on the line. I didn't think about doing this, I just did it. It was a lifeline to the outside, and I wanted to keep it open. I knew the gunman couldn't see the phone behind the counter of the front desk, and I guess that's why I felt okay doing it. God knows what would have happened if he saw the call light blinking.

"Now call a news station," he barked.

"Okay," I said. "Which news station?" I was so scared I couldn't even think of a place to call. I was drawing a blank.

"Call a news station," the gunman repeated.

"I don't have a number," I said. "Do you know the number?"

"Yeah, I have the number," he said, but he didn't tell me what it was.

Instead he sat on the chair and opened his black backpack and took out a small bottle of water. He unscrewed the cap, took a long drink, and put the cap back on. Then he reached into his backpack again. This time he pulled out something black and bulky.

It was a magazine that held bullets for his AK-47.

The gunman went to work, methodically, like he'd rehearsed this many times before in the quiet of a bedroom. He reached into his backpack and pulled out a handful of loose bullets, and he loaded them into the magazine. When he filled it he put it down and reached for another magazine, and scooped up another handful of bullets and filled that magazine, too. He filled either four or five magazines, I can't remember, and then he reached into the backpack and pulled out more big handfuls of loose bullets and

69

stuffed them into the pockets of his pants. He kept stuffing more bullets in until his pockets were bulging.

During the gunman's reloading ritual I heard my cell phone vibrate.

I looked up to see if the gunman had noticed, but he hadn't. Silently I thanked God I had my phone on vibrate. The rule at McNair is that teachers and staffers must keep their cells on vibrate at all times, but of course we don't always remember to do that. But thankfully, on that day, I remembered. If I hadn't and my phone had sounded, who knows what the gunman might have done.

> THE GUNMAN WENT TO WORK, METHODICALLY, LIKE HE'D REHEARSED THIS MANY TIMES.

Very discreetly I looked down at my cell. It was a text message from one of the teachers in the building.

"Is this for real?" the message read.

The teacher heard my announcement over the intercom. Maybe she even heard the shooting. Still her brain couldn't fully process what was happening because it was too terrible to be true. I understood that. I didn't want the gunman to see me on my phone, so very carefully I typed in just three letters.

"Y-E-S."

I looked up at the gunman. He had crammed the last of his bullets into his pockets. Hundreds of them, by what I could tell. Then he took his rifle and pulled out the empty magazine and dropped it to the floor. He took one of the loaded magazines and snapped it onto the rifle. It locked in place with a crisp, metallic sound. I will never forget that sound.

The gunman was ready now. Whatever his mission was, he was prepared to end it.

///

WE ARE TROUBLED ON EVERY SIDE,
YET NOT DISTRESSED; WE ARE
PERPLEXED, BUT NOT IN DESPAIR;
PERSECUTED, BUT NOT FORSAKEN;
CAST DOWN, BUT NOT DESTROYED.

2 Corinthians 4:8–9

///

CHAPTER FOUR

Tuesday, August 20, 2013

I am standing in the shadow of death and all around me is darkness and chaos and in the midst of it all I think, *No, it cannot be this way. We must not die today, we must survive. We must go home to our families, we must kiss our loved ones. We must live so that we can serve God.*

I think, *The Devil shall lay no claim to our souls this day.*

But how do you bring the light of life to a room that reeks of death? How do you battle pocketsful of bullets, a mind determined to die? What is stronger in our hearts—faith or fear?

The truth is, I had only one weapon at my disposal, and that weapon was my words.

I was going through a time in my life when my words did not seem to matter. When nothing I said seemed to make much difference to anyone—when my pleas and my dreams went unanswered, or so, at least, it seemed. A time when no one in the world was listening to me, or at least that's how it felt.

But of course, someone *was* listening. Someone always is.

Now suddenly, without the slightest warning, I was in a situation where every word out of my mouth might be the difference between living and dying. Where my words were not just important, they were the *most* important thing of all. So on this day every word must be uttered with accuracy, with care, because the smallest mix-up or mistranslation might spell doom—not just for me but for hundreds of souls.

So how could I be sure that every word out of my mouth would be measured? How could I make sure every word counted?

It is right there in Psalm 141:3: "Set a watch, O Lord, before my mouth; keep the door of my lips."

God would set a guard. He would keep the door. All I had to do was listen. Because if ever there was a day when I needed to free up my ears and listen to what He was telling me, *this* was that day.

The problem is, I wasn't always very good at freeing up my ears. I wasn't very good at listening. All of us are good at talking, but sometimes we're not so great at hearing the words that come back. I mean *really* hearing them. Yet that's the only way we can have a true conversation with anybody—by spending as much time listening as talking. Otherwise we're just babbling to ourselves.

The same is true of our conversations with God.

Listening to God was something I had to work on. The troubles in my life—the ones I have described so far and the ones I've yet to tell—forced me to stop talking and start listening. It was my spiritual mentor, Apostle Tuff, who helped me on that journey.

Dr. Ulysses Tuff is Terry's uncle, and he pastors my church in Atlanta. Apostle Tuff has the biggest heart of anyone I know. He's in his sixties, but he's still a young man, and he rides his bike for miles and miles on the trails near his home. He shows no favoritism, except to God. Doesn't matter if you're a millionaire or a two-dollar person, Apostle Tuff will treat you the same. God comes first. All the rest of us come second.

Apostle Tuff is the one who taught me about quiet time.

The idea was to set up times in my life when I could have a quiet, meaningful conversation with God. And the crazier my life was, the more quiet time I needed. When things are chaotic, that's exactly when you need God's guidance the most. So I had to train myself to clear my head even when the world around me was crumbling, so that God's words could come through and lead me to still waters.

In the weeks before August 20, my training began.

Apostle Tuff had me focus on 1 Corinthians 15:58: "Therefore, my beloved brethren, be ye steadfast, unmovable, always abounding in the work of the Lord, forasmuch as ye know that your labor is not in vain." *Steadfast* and *unmovable*—those two words stayed with me. My life was a roller coaster of pain and anger and despair and dejection, but inside I could remain steadfast and unmovable in the Lord. It was possible to do—I just had to find a way to do it.

The trick, it turned out, was practice. At night I began going to sleep with an audiobook of the Bible playing softly by my bed. I would lay there and listen to the words of the Bible and let them wash over me, and I would drift off to sleep with a wonderful feeling of peace and safety. I'd get up at 5:00 a.m., go down to the kitchen, and put on a CD of jazz versions of gospel songs like "To Worship You," and I'd sit at the table and talk to God. Not praying, just talking, out loud, into the air. If I got up to make coffee I'd keep talking, as if God were right there next to me, having breakfast. Sometimes I'd talk so loud I'd hear one of my kids yell out, "Mom, be quiet, you're talking to God too loud!"

Most days I probably talked to God for a good fifteen minutes. I'd tell Him what's happening, ask Him questions, work things out. Now, Apostle taught me that for as long as you talk to God, *that's how long you have to listen.* So if I talked for fifteen minutes, then I had to sit at the table in total silence and just listen for fifteen minutes. I'd close my eyes and shut everything down and block out the world as best I could, and I would sit there and listen.

That's quiet time.

Trust me, sitting still for fifteen minutes isn't as easy as it sounds. I could sit and watch a TV show for an hour, but listening for the Lord for fifteen minutes was a challenge. I had to work on it. I had to practice. Especially when there were a million things I had to do, a million things going through my mind. But it was worth the effort—"your labor is not in vain," the Bible says. I had to train myself to be steadfast and unmovable, and then I could abound in the work of the Lord.

Most days God did not answer me during my quiet time. That's just the way it is. But some days He'd guide me to a Scripture and I'd open my Bible and read His words, and those words were *always* a response to something I asked Him about. One particularly terrible morning, when I felt my life was so out of control it was hardly worth living, God directed me to Psalm 118:17–18:

"I shall not die, but live, and declare the works of the Lord," it read. "The Lord has chastened me severely, but He has not given me over to death" (NKJV).

I started to weep. It was God's answer to me, and it made me feel so safe. No, *I will not die*—I will live so that I can serve Him. How much clearer could God's answer be?

And yet, if I hadn't had my quiet time—if I hadn't shut out the chaos and just listened—I might not have heard God's words. That happens to us all the time. We're too busy or too distracted or too frightened to hear what He is telling us. But now I was training myself to stay calm and free my ears, so that God's words could come to me smoothly and easily, in any situation—no matter how chaotic or frightening it might be.

/////

"Okay, I found a news channel," I said to the gunman—pretending, I guess, that I hadn't just watched him stuff hundreds of bullets in his pockets. "Here is Channel 2 News. Do you want me to call them?" I'd just finished searching for a news station on Google, and the first one that came up was Channel 2.

"Yes, call them," the gunman said.

I dialed the number. A woman answered.

"I have a man here with a gun," I said. "At the Ronald E. McNair Discovery Learning Academy."

The gunman took a step toward me.

"Tell them I want a news helicopter."

"He said he wants a news helicopter here."

"Tell them I want them to record the incident."

I repeated his words.

"I want them to see what I'm doing blow by blow."

"He wants you to see everything he's going to do, blow by blow."

"Okay, hang up," the gunman said.

I lowered the phone to where he couldn't see it and once again I pressed the hold button. Then, instead of putting the receiver in its cradle, I quietly laid it on the desk, where he couldn't see it. Then I pressed the first hold button again.

The line to the police was open. The 9-1-1 dispatcher would be able to hear everything that happened in the room.

The gunman went back to pacing. At least he wasn't in any hurry to start shooting again. I tried to remind myself that the boy came in talking, not shooting. As well as I could remember, in other shootings it was almost always the other way around.

"What is your name?" I asked him again.

Again, he didn't answer.

Instead he reached into his book bag, looking for something. He pulled out a cell phone and dialed a number. I said nothing and just let him make his call.

"I have done something really bad," he said when someone picked up, "and I know I'm going to have to pay for it."

The shooter was silent as the other person spoke. I imagine they were asking, "What in the world did you do?"

"I'm at the school," the gunman said. "I'm the person on the news. They're going to kill me because of what I did. I shot at the police."

I surprised myself by jumping into the conversation.

"No, it's okay, they're not going to kill you," I said. "You didn't harm anybody." I couldn't be sure this was true, but I said it anyway to try and calm him down.

"You don't understand," he said to me, "I shot at the police."

"That don't make any difference," I said. "You might have shot at them, but you didn't harm no one."

I heard an urgent voice come through his cell phone. Whoever it was sounded frightened and desperate.

"Don't do it!!" they were saying. "*Don't do it!*"

But the gunman wasn't listening. He was drifting off into his own world again. I tried to pull him back.

> I HEARD AN URGENT VOICE COME THROUGH HIS CELL PHONE. WHOEVER IT WAS SOUNDED FRIGHTENED AND DESPERATE.

"Do you want me to contact anyone and tell them you didn't harm me?" I said. "I'll tell them you didn't hurt anyone, and everything is going to be okay."

"You don't understand," the gunman said, his voice rising with anger. "*I am going to die today.*"

Just then I heard my cell phone vibrate again. I looked down quickly to see who it was. My heart sank when I saw the name. It was my daughter, LaVita.

Someone from the school must have called her and told her what was happening. She would know I was likely in the front of the school, near as anyone to where the gunman came in. Maybe she'd even already imagined I was dead. That was why she was calling—to hear my voice, to know I was still alive.

But I couldn't answer her call. I couldn't risk the gunman seeing me on the phone. All I could do was let it ring until the call ended. It killed me to leave LaVita hanging like that. But I had to ignore her call.

I heard the frightened voice come through the gunman's cell again.

"Don't do it! Please don't do it."

The gunman ended the call and angrily threw his phone back in his bag. He was fuming and restless now, his face red, his hands tight around his gun, his body lurching from spot to spot. The demon inside him was winning.

And if that had been someone who loved him on the other end of the call—and surely there was someone out there in the world who did—then they, too, had been left hanging, just like my daughter. They, too, were left to fight off their most unthinkable fears. They had no way of knowing if and when death would come for the person they loved—hours from now? Five minutes from now? This very second?

I had no way of knowing, either. Only God and the gunman knew.

/////

Sometimes when I was home and in my bath, I'd hear the sound of a soft voice coming through the door.

It was my young son Derrick, sitting just outside and singing some silly song he'd made up for me and keeping rhythm by playing drums with his hands on the floor. From very early on he loved to sing and keep the beat, as if he was always hearing beautiful music no one else could hear. That's why, if someone asked me about Derrick, I would say he was a musician at heart. His songs to me were his way of telling me he loved me. So I'd sit in the bathtub and just listen to him sing.

Whenever I was around Derrick I tried to be steadfast and strong—tried not to let him see how bad I felt because of his struggles. But I'm afraid I didn't always succeed. There were times I'd watch him have a hard time walking or eating and my heart would just break apart, and Terry would know I was sad for him.

But, like I said, God may have given my son weak legs and bad eyes, but He also gave him the spirit of a champion. God made him a fighter. So even as his muscles and his nerves were deteriorating, his heart just kept getting bigger. And when I was weak, Derrick was strong enough for both of us. He would know when I was down and he would rub my head and sing to me, or maybe he'd just hug me and hold me and tell me a funny little story. He was always there to pick me up when I needed it most, and somehow he always knew just the right words to say to fix what was broken.

That has never changed.

Yet there was one important thing I could do for Derrick, and it became my mission to do it. One day when Derrick was young and surrounded by therapists, I closed my eyes and formed a picture of him as a grown-up. I saw him on a street corner, in tattered clothes, leaning on a cane and begging for bread. I opened my eyes and vowed to never have that vision again. I went to my Bible and found a passage from 2 Thessalonians 3:10: "For even when we were with you, this we commanded you, that if any would not work, neither should he eat."

Those words became the guiding force behind my mission—to prepare Derrick for the world. I would not see him or treat him as disabled, and I would push him not to see himself that way either. I didn't care how many therapists he had to work with. I did not want him to ever become reliant on them.

> GOD MAY HAVE GIVEN MY SON WEAK LEGS AND BAD EYES, BUT HE ALSO GAVE HIM THE SPIRIT OF A CHAMPION.

"People are not going to do things for you your whole life," I told him. "You're going to have to do them for yourself, or else they won't get done."

Sometimes Derrick wouldn't like how hard I pushed him to be self-sufficient, but that was okay. "I'm just training you for your wife," I'd explain. Part of treating Derrick like any other child was not being afraid to discipline him, and his father and I never gave him special treatment when it came to punishment. When Derrick got older and was diagnosed with ADHD, and his behavior sometimes got out of hand, I drew up a contract with both my children. It was simple: in one column was the misbehavior, and across from it was the punishment. "If you do this or that," I told them, "these are the consequences." I had both of them sign their contracts, and they kept a copy in their rooms.

So whenever Derrick did something bad, all I had to say was, "Go see your contract." Derrick had a habit of using his hands to beat tempo all the time, on the floor or a table or his desk or wherever, and sometimes he would do it during teaching time or in class. Suddenly you'd hear drumming, and you'd know Derrick was off in his own world. It was like he had a whole band playing in his head. I loved his musicality, but I knew he needed to understand he couldn't disrupt a class or a meal just because he felt like pounding out a beat.

So on his contract, in the Misbehavior column, I wrote, "Playing Drums Thing." The consequence was not being allowed to eat with the family when we went to a restaurant. Now, there were few things Derrick enjoyed more than going out to eat, so that was a serious punishment. Even so we stuck to it, and Derrick would come with us to the restaurant and just sit there while we ate, and then I'd cook him dinner when we got home. This punishment only happened a couple of times, because, you know, eating was my son's favorite hobby.

Sometimes Derrick spoke rudely to a teacher, and the punishment for that was not being able to talk to me for a few minutes. Derrick hated disappointing me, and he hated not being able to talk to me, even for a short time. But when he spoke rudely I'd say, "Mommy can't talk to you right now because of your behavior." I could barely stand to see him follow me around hoping I'd start talking, but a contract was a contract. Better he learn now not to be rude and not when the consequences would be worse.

The harshest punishment of all, however, was the time-out. Derrick *hated* time-outs. He had so much energy and such a love of life, for him sitting quietly in a corner for twenty minutes must have felt like twenty hours. Seeing how deflated he was to have to sit still for so long wasn't an easy thing to watch. None of the punishments were easy for me to hand out. But I believed it was my job to get my son ready to be on his own in the world. If I wanted him to live a normal life, he needed to know what a normal life looked like.

I had one other unbreakable rule—I never left Derrick alone at home just because it would have been easier to do something without him. I didn't want him sitting around idle-minded. I didn't want him to live his life in a bubble. So wherever I went I took him with me. That was the unbreakable rule: "Where I go, you go."

"Come on, son, we're going shopping."

"I'm coming too, Mommy?"

"Where I go, you go."

When he was in elementary school, I enrolled Derrick in special ed classes. I figured that with all the other therapy he had to do, keeping up with the mainstream kids might be too hard for him. But after a while I saw Derrick wasn't being pushed hard enough at school. He wasn't excited about his classes, and he came home with the same assignments week after week. For instance, when he was in the sixth grade he was on the same lesson—about the rain forest—for more than six weeks! I went to see his teacher and asked why it was taking so long to learn about the rain forest.

"Ain't that much rain and ain't that much forest," I said.

But it was clear the teachers didn't think the kids were smart enough to go any faster.

About that time I found out that Derrick wouldn't be able to apply for college with a special education diploma. I decided to start dropping in on his classes to see for myself if he really needed to be in special ed. On my first surprise visit I walked in on Derrick and another student slumped on a sofa doing drumbeats while the teacher was nowhere to be found. I didn't allow my son to sit around on the sofa all day long at home, and I sure wasn't going to let him do it at school. I marched right down to the principal's office and demanded he let my son be mainstreamed.

Derrick never took another special ed class again.

I pushed my daughter, LaVita, just as hard, maybe even harder.

As I told you, I dropped out of high school and never went to college, and I had my first baby when I was twenty. My mother had me when she was just a teenager. None of the men on my mother's side and very few men on my father's side had been successful—mostly they were alcoholics, drug addicts, or prisoners. The same was true of the women in our past—few had been able to rise above their station. I knew what all this meant.

My children were facing a generational curse.

"The Lord is slow to anger and filled with unfailing love, forgiving every kind of sin and rebellion," it says in Numbers 14:18, "but he does not excuse the guilty. He lays the sins of the parents upon their children; the entire family is affected—even children in the third and fourth generations" (NLT). Unless you lived your life in Christ—unless you lived it the *right* way—the sins of the father and the mother would be visited on you. Their sins would become your sins.

It was up to my children to break this curse.

Was I asking too much of them? Can we expect our youngsters to shrug off the sins of their ancestors and break free from burdens they don't even understand? I was under no delusion it would be easy. But I did believe it was possible. And I believed my kids could do it.

Why? Because the blueprint is right there in the Bible.

I taught my children how to do things I believed would help them break the curse. One of them was recognizing the power of their words. "So I say to you, ask, and it will be given to you," it says in Luke 11:9. "Seek, and you will find; knock, and it will be opened to you" (NKJV). God wants us to speak out and give voice to our dreams and goals. We must not just think them, as if we only half-believe in them. We must speak them aloud to make them happen. It is our words that give evidence of our faith. And it is our dreams that give glory to God. "Think clearly and exercise self-control. Look forward to the gracious salvation that will come to you when Jesus Christ is revealed to the world," it says in 1 Peter 1:13 (NLT). I wanted to prepare my children to win the battle of their futures, and I wanted them to set their hope fully on God's grace. I wanted them to understand the power of their words.

Most of all, I tried to teach them that it was in their will to break the curse. They had the means to do it, as long as they exerted their will on the world. They couldn't be passive. They couldn't make excuses. They couldn't wait for someone else to open doors for them. They had to be strong and determined. And they had to push open those doors themselves. "Behold, I stand at the door and knock," it says in Revelation 3:20. "If anyone hears My voice and opens the door, I will come in to him and dine with him, and he with Me" (NKJV). God is always there, beckoning us to come. But we have to open the door ourselves. God is not going to carry us through. We have to exert our will and get through on our own.

I wanted my children to understand the great gift Jesus gave us all by dying on the cross. And I wanted them to know they could break the generational curse. But I also wanted them to know I would be with them every step of the way, making sure they didn't forget what I taught them.

"All them women before you had babies before they got diplomas, and they ended up in abusive marriages," I told La Vita more than once. "You cannot let that be your testimony."

La Vita was smart as a whip and had the same fighting spirit as me. I just wanted her to find the right outlet for it. So when she was young I signed her up for debate class.

It worked.

In middle school La Vita was not only the best debater on her school team, she was named the number one debater for her age in the whole state. In high school she became a national champion. Every few weeks she would bring another ribbon or another trophy home. With every new prize she broke the curse a little bit more.

Yet I understood that to really break the curse, La Vita would have to go to college. Early on, when she was still in elementary school, Terry and I redecorated her bedroom while she was away at school. We got new sheets and pillowcases and bedspreads, all with the logo of the University of Kentucky, which I knew was one of the top schools in the country. We got Kentucky U pennants and posters and put them on the walls. College was still years away for LaVita, but what we were doing was planting seeds. "He shall be like a tree planted by the waters, which spreads out its roots by the river," it says in Jeremiah 17:8. It "will not fear when heat comes; but its leaf will be green, and will not be anxious in the year of drought, nor will cease from yielding fruit" (NKJV). The seeds we were planting now, we hoped, would make LaVita strong and powerful down the road.

When she came home from school the day we redecorated, we led her to her closed bedroom door and paused before she went in.

"Walk into your destiny," I said.

LaVita burst in and squealed. She loved her shiny new bedroom. And years later, when the time came, LaVita did enroll in college—not at the University of Kentucky but at Tennessee State University. That was fine by me, because it meant she was well on her way to breaking the curse.

LaVita made the university's forensics team, which focused on the competitive art of public speaking, and she started coming home with trophies again. Before she graduated, she even competed on the team that placed in the top five internationally.

One New Year's holiday my mother-in-law called us and said she wasn't feeling well, so we packed up our family and drove to her house in Washington DC. When we arrived we could tell something was wrong. Terry's mother looked tired and not well at all. We soon discovered she had cancer. The doctors gave her only a few months to live, so we moved her down to Macon, Georgia, which was her home.

I told Terry he should go be with his mother, and I would stay behind with the kids until they finished school that year. When they did, we got a big U-Haul, hitched it to our old green Nissan Sentra, packed in all our stuff and drove to Macon. Terry's aunt let us stay in a rental house she owned, and she fixed it up and we lived there for two years. I was making money braiding hair—I was so good at it I could charge eighty dollars a braiding—and Terry was working for the city of Macon. After two years we moved to Atlanta, where the jobs were better. I did temporary administrative work and Terry got hired as a maintenance man by the top black-owned construction company in Atlanta.

The move to Georgia helped Derrick the most. On top of his regular school we signed him up for two classes a week at the Center for the Visually Impaired (CVI) and the National Federation of the Blind in Atlanta. That's where he really began to thrive. He met other kids with problems similar to his, and they became his best friends in the world. Because he was so smart, he even became an advocate for other disabled kids, going to different events and talking about the challenges they faced. He loved traveling with his friends to outings and events all over the state, and for the first time he got an idea of what life would be like without his momma around.

His first year in high school, though, was a setback. Derrick told me his teachers were treating him differently from the other students, and some of them were even harping on his disabilities. There was only one teacher he liked—one teacher who treated him normally—and midway through his freshman year that teacher got transferred to another class. I could tell Derrick was starting to feel defeated by it all. The passion and excitement he felt when he was at the Center for the Visually Impaired had disappeared.

Then one Christmas Day, we were at the family house with Apostle Tuff for Christmas dinner. I knew Derrick had been spending time with Apostle, and I thought that was good for him. I knew Apostle to be a strong, decent, good-hearted man. I was happy he and Derrick got to talk so much, because the truth is, Derrick and his father didn't talk all that much at all.

During the dinner Derrick turned to Apostle and said, "I want you to tell my momma about me going to school in Macon."

I had no idea what he was referring to. I'd never heard a word about this before. Macon was more than eighty miles from where we lived. So how in the world was he going to go to school there?

The only two words that came out of my mouth were, "Oh, no."

Apostle Tuff explained everything to me. He said Derrick wanted to go to the Georgia Academy for the Blind in Macon. From his time at CVI, Derrick knew lots of people at the academy, and he wanted to enroll full-time. That meant he would have to stay over in Macon, which meant he would have to leave home. I could not get my mind around that. Yes, I had prepared Derrick to live without me.

But I hadn't prepared myself to live without him.

I resisted the idea and told Apostle and Derrick all the reasons it wouldn't work. Apostle was gentle with me, but firm.

I had prepared
Derrick to live
without me. But I
hadn't prepared
myself to live
without him.

"Marie," he said, "you know you're going to have to let him go."

"He's my baby," I protested.

"Marie, you gotta let him go."

I knew he was right, but I still put up a fight until finally admitting I should let Derrick go.

That August, Derrick started classes at the Georgia Academy. A yellow school bus would pick him up on Sunday evenings and drive him to the campus, where he would spend the week. Then the bus would bring him back home on Friday. That was going to be the deal for the next three years.

I will never forget the first Sunday they came to take my son away.

I got up early, as always, and cooked Derrick his usual IHOP breakfast, and we spent most of that day together, talking, laughing, hugging, singing, doing all the stuff we do. As the day wore on I felt more and more depressed. I tried to hide my feelings, but it was almost impossible. Finally it was time to get Derrick ready to go. We dressed him in a pair of jeans and a crisp white shirt, and I packed a bag with clothes and supplies. Then he sat in his wheelchair in the living room and waited for the bus to come.

I looked at my beautiful son as he sat there and I felt my lower lip start to tremble. I tried to bite it, but that did no good. Soon a whole wave of emotion came washing over me.

Derrick could not walk. The muscles in his legs were all but gone. He would always be in a wheelchair. The nerves in his hands were badly damaged. His head and neck were still not right. He was legally blind.

Yet his heart and his spirit and his soul were pure and perfect. His mind was alive and beautiful. He loved God, and he rejoiced in the church, and he did not act as if he lacked for anything. He never felt sorry for himself. He was so much stronger and braver than I would ever be. I loved that boy with every ounce of my being and I wished him every happiness God would grant to him.

I just didn't want to see him go.

Only a few weeks earlier I had turned forty. LaVita was away at college full-time. Terry had a long haul bus-driving job that kept him away from the house for six days straight. And now my baby was leaving, too. Soon as they put him on that bus, I would be alone.

Before long the bus driver pulled up, and Derrick heard him through the window. I could see how excited he was. But as soon as I let the driver into the house, I lost it. I started crying and I couldn't stop. I felt the deep, familiar ache and sadness of being abandoned—like when I realized my father didn't care about me, like when Terry gave my ring to another woman, like when Momma wouldn't let me move in with her. Derrick was doing nothing wrong; in fact, he was doing everything right, just like I'd taught him to do. But even so, I already missed him so very much I wanted to throw myself on the ground and grab hold of his wheelchair and never let go.

I know I should have been strong and resolute for Derrick's sake, but I just couldn't be. So, as usual, he was the one who was strong and resolute for me.

He wheeled over to me and hugged me around the waist.

"Mommy, it's going to be okay," he said.

I kept crying. I couldn't help it.

"Don't worry, Mommy," he said, hugging me tighter, "you won't ever be alone. The Father, the Son, and the Holy Ghost are gonna be in the house with you every day."

I stopped crying. I leaned down and kissed him on the forehead. My son was ready to separate from me. I had prepared him for this. Now it was time for him to go. The driver pushed him out the front door and I heard Derrick say one last thing to me before he went.

"I love you, Mommy."

"I love you too, baby."

Then the front door closed.

/////

"The Lord is nigh unto them that are of a broken heart; and saveth such as be of a contrite spirit." So it says in Psalm 34:18. God is telling us that just when everything seems lost—just when we feel *most* alone—that's when He moves nearest to us. You see, my son was right. I was not alone. My house *was* crowded with God.

And then, out of the blue, I got a phone call from my father. He was calling to apologize for the bad things he did to me when I was a little girl. He said he was sorry for all the hurt and all the pain. I was surprised to hear from him, but I told him I forgave him. It was an unexpected blessing—and God's way of showing me I wasn't alone in the world.

What happened next, though, was something I never expected, and it would be the hardest trial I ever went through—a trial I wasn't sure I would survive.

It was enough to make me stop believing God was anywhere near me. When it happened I dug deep into my Bible, searching for a way to keep believing in God's mercy, but the truth is, there were times when I just didn't. The words of the Bible became just words. The Lord's message was lost.

"God is our refuge and strength, a very present help in trouble," it says in Psalm 46:1–3. "Therefore we will not fear, even though the earth be removed, and though the mountains be carried into the midst of the sea; though its waters roar and be troubled, though the mountains shake with its swelling" (NKJV).

But after what happened next in my life, I *did* fear.

Because, in my life, the mountains shook.

//

I WILL CALL ON THE LORD, WHO IS
WORTHY TO BE PRAISED: SO SHALL
I BE SAVED FROM MINE ENEMIES.

2 Samuel 22:4

//

CHAPTER FIVE

Tuesday, August 20, 2013

The gunman had fully armed himself with loaded magazines and hundreds of bullets, as if getting ready for one last stand. He was back to pacing maniacally, his body fighting his mind. Outside the school I guessed there were probably dozens of police officers and SWAT members and state troopers, aiming their weapons right at the window of the front office—right where the gunman and I were holed up, behind just the glass and the thin material of the window blinds. I couldn't hear them, but I knew TV and police helicopters had to be circling overhead. This quiet little street in a quiet neighborhood was bracing for all-out war.

And in the middle of it all one thought, one concern, kept coming back to me, no matter how much I tried to ignore it.

I really had to pee.

I didn't think I'd be able to hold it any longer. The pressure was just too much. I already had to go before all this started, and now the terror in my bones was making it unbearable. The lyrics of an old Shirley Caesar gospel song began jumping in and out of my head. The song is called "Hold My Mule," which is a southern saying that means, roughly, Lord, give me some restraint. I guess that's why that song popped in my mind—because, Lord knows, I needed to hold my mule. In the song, Shirley sings about praising God all day long, and I sang along with her in my mind, which helped me forget how much I had to go to the bathroom. But only some of the time.

I guess it hardly mattered if I peed myself or not. Wasn't anyone who wouldn't understand if I did. But for whatever reason I just didn't want to. It became important to me *not* to.

So I did something that, if I'd thought about it a little longer, I maybe wouldn't have done.

While the gunman was huffing and puffing and pacing, I calmly asked . . .

"Can I go to the bathroom?"

The gunman stopped pacing. He didn't look at me—he still hadn't made eye contact. But he did turn in my direction.

"Where's the bathroom?" he asked.

"It's right down the hallway," I said.

He thought about it for another moment, then said, "Yeah, okay."

I got up from my chair. My legs still felt like jelly. But here was another chance for me to make a break for it. If I got out of the front office, maybe I'd be able to scramble to safety somewhere. I can't say that's the reason I asked him if I could go—the reason was that I really had to *go*—but when he gave me permission, the thought of getting away from him overcame the thought of having to pee.

And yet, once again, I did not move. Once again, my legs stayed right where they were. Before I could take a single step it occurred to me like a lightning bolt that if I went into the hallway *he might follow me*. And that would put him just a few feet away from where the children were. In a way I would be leading him right to them. It wasn't like I was having these separate thoughts one after the other, then processing them and making a decision. There was no time for all that. Basically I went from knowing I had to go to the bathroom or else I would pee myself, to knowing there was no way I could go. I had to stay in the front office, with the gunman. If I peed myself, well, then, so be it. But I had to keep the gunman here, away from the kids.

Something else occurred to me in that moment.

I HAD TO KEEP THE GUNMAN HERE, AWAY FROM THE KIDS.

It was almost ridiculous that in the middle of a violent standoff I asked the gunman if I could go to the bathroom. If I had heard someone else did that I might have thought, *How dumb can you be?*

But what was even more surprising was that the gunman said yes. The gunman was willing to let me go.

We hadn't even looked each other in the eye. We didn't know each other's names. We'd spent less than an hour in each other's lives. And we were on opposite sides of a very dangerous battle.

And yet, somehow, some kind of bond was forming between us. The gunman had let two other people go, but he'd kept me in the room with him. Why? I had no way of knowing. But maybe it was because he saw something in me that made him trust me. Something unspoken, something other people might not see. Something maybe only someone in his position *could* see. So when I asked him if I could go to the bathroom, he said yes.

In that instant, in the unlikeliest of settings, the gunman had shown me a tiny bit of compassion.

Whatever drove him to do that, however, disappeared in a flash, because no sooner had I decided I couldn't go to the bathroom, the gunman, suddenly agitated, reached for the plastic chair again. I knew what that meant. He yanked on the front door of the office and used the chair to prop it open. He stepped toward the front entrance to the school. He raised his gun to a shooting position. From my desk I once again saw him push open one of the entrance doors.

Then I heard the thunder. The gunman was shooting again.

After LaVita went away to college and Derrick went to Macon for high school, something happened in my life that changed everything. It had to do with Terry.

Now, Terry was a good husband to me. We had known each other going on thirty years, since we were both kids, and most of that time he was caring and attentive, and as far as I could tell he always put me first. He came home from work to my children and

me every day, like clockwork. Maybe he wasn't the most emotionally open man in the world, and there were times when I worried
he wasn't spending enough time with LaVita and Derrick, particularly Derrick, and I told him so. And he would try to spend
more time with them, and if that seemed to be a chore to him I
didn't notice, at least not then. Because, as I said, I believed in
him. I believed he was a good man.

Terry knew that no matter what, I would take care of him.
He knew he would always come home to a clean house and a
hot meal and freshly washed clothes and every other comfort he
desired. And he knew that if some matter of the family had to
be handled, I would handle it. It got to where we were not two
people but one, and I would pick up his checks from work and
sign them for him and use the money to pay the bills and maybe
buy myself something once in a while, and Terry didn't mind.
As long as I was happy he was happy, and even though we didn't
have much money, no one could tell me I wasn't in heaven, because
that's what Terry made me feel like most days—like I was smack
dab in heaven.

Every now and then Terry and I went on vacations with the
kids. One year we even went by ourselves, just the two of us,
to the eastern Caribbean. And back home we went shopping
together and we went to restaurants together and we went to
church together, and we slept and prayed and ate and rested and
laughed and cried together. And when the children got older
and went away to school, I told Terry this was our time now. We
started doing even more things together, going on dates, going to
movies, trying new restaurants, and I believed our love for each

other deepened, and for years and years after our wedding we still held hands.

There was no space between us. We were in this life together. But all that changed.

It did not happen suddenly. It was gradual. It was just something I began to notice over time. For instance, we stopped holding hands. We did fewer things together, and more things on our own. When he came home from work we would say hello and eat dinner, but then I would go upstairs and instead of coming with me he would stay downstairs. He might spend hours down there, watching TV and doing other things. One Sunday morning, out of the blue, he broke a tradition we had stuck to since the early days.

"I'm not going to church today," Terry said. "Go without me."

"Why aren't you going?"

"Just don't want to. I'm tired."

Around that time a sickening feeling began coming over me. A feeling of uneasiness and anxiety, maybe even panic. I only knew one way to live, and that was with Terry. He was the only man I'd ever been with, the only man in the world I *could* be with. For nearly as long as I could remember, there wasn't a Terry and an Antoinette, there was just the two of us, together, in everything, forever. In my mind there was no possibility of anything else. A life without Terry might as well be a life without a beating heart.

And yet I could not deny the truth of what was happening to us. Terry and I had become spiritually disconnected.

I suppose this happens to a lot of couples—they start pulling apart. Maybe that's just human nature, I don't know. Maybe what was happening to me was something a lot of women go through, and maybe a lot of them just pick up and move on. I'm not trying to turn my situation into some kind of great tragedy. Looking at it from the outside, you might say it wasn't the end of the world.

But to me, losing Terry *was* the end of my world.

Not to sound too dramatic, but I truly had no idea how or even if I could survive without him. And besides, we'd spent most of our lives together, and that kind of commitment is not something you just throw out with the trash. A marriage is sacred; we swear to it before God. "Have you not read that He who made them at the beginning 'made them male and female,' and said, 'For this reason a man shall leave his father and mother and be joined to his wife, and the two shall become one flesh'?" it says in Matthew 19:4–6. "Therefore what God has joined together, let not man separate" (NKJV).

If Terry was pulling away from me, then that was the truth of it. It was just something I'd have to deal with. But in my mind there was only one solution to our problem—we had to fix whatever was broken. We had to find a way to become close again.

One morning, after cooking Terry breakfast, I told him I wanted to meet him for lunch.

"What for?" he said.

"There's a disconnection between us," I said. "We're pulling apart. We need to talk about it and do something about it."

Terry agreed to go to lunch at the coffee shop at the Northlake Mall. This would be our come-to-Jesus lunch. When we got there he slumped in his chair and made a face, as if this was the last place he wanted to be—but at least he was there. I spoke my piece. I told him what I thought was happening. I asked for his opinion.

"Something is wrong," he said.

We spent the next hour talking about our marriage and our lives. It was like we were trying to rediscover the purpose of our being together. "I never had a relationship with anyone else but you," he said at one point. "I don't even know what a relationship is supposed to be." That admission didn't alarm me. In fact, I felt good that at least Terry was opening up. He was feeling the same disconnect I was. And that meant he would want to figure out a way to fix it, same as me.

After that, we spent time with Terry's aunt, a smart and wonderful woman who gave us advice about marriage. She became our unofficial marriage counselor. I also spoke a lot with Apostle Tuff. In one of my talks with him, it began to dawn on me that no one had ever taught me what it means to be a good wife. Not my mother, and certainly not my father. It was Apostle Tuff who made me realize that there was something I could do to pull Terry back to me. It was right there in the Bible. "An excellent wife," it says in Proverbs 31:10–12, "is far more precious than jewels. The heart of her husband trusts in her, and he will have no lack of gain. She does him good, and not harm, all the days of her life" (ESV).

I could do something good for my husband. I could make him see what an excellent wife he had.

✂✂✂✂✂

I COULD DO
SOMETHING GOOD
FOR MY HUSBAND. I
COULD MAKE HIM SEE
WHAT AN EXCELLENT
WIFE HE HAD.

We didn't have much money in those days—Terry was driving a bus and I was working as a bookkeeper for the DeKalb County school district, and everything we earned went toward keeping the family afloat. I decided to take a second job to make some extra money, so I signed up as a sponsor with a group called Cool Girls—an after-school program devoted to young, troubled girls. I loved working with those girls, especially now that my own babies were both away. And the extra money allowed me to go forward with my big plan—a fourteen-day getaway drive for Terry and me to celebrate our twenty-first wedding anniversary.

I spent months planning the trip down to the last detail. From Atlanta down to Dallas, then to San Antonio, and from there to Phoenix and finally Las Vegas. After two nights in a suite at the MGM Grand we'd drive back home through Albuquerque and Memphis. It would be like the old days—just Terry and me, doing something fun together. It would be our chance to spiritually reconnect.

"This is all about you and me having time for each other," I told him. "God said this is where He is taking us in our new life together."

The trip started out really well. We hopped in our midsize car and drove west, stopping at a mall, doing a little sightseeing, and taking a boat ride in San Antonio. After that we walked by the river holding hands. It felt good to me to be holding hands with Terry again. The next morning I'd arranged for the chef where we were staying to cook us a special breakfast. The chef even came out to introduce himself, and it was one of the nicest meals we ever shared. It seemed to me like Terry was really enjoying himself.

He was relaxed and attentive. And there were so many more good moments to come, or so I thought.

Our next stop was Dallas, where once again I'd arranged for a chef to cook us a special breakfast. But as I was getting dressed to go down to the restaurant, I noticed Terry wasn't getting ready.

"Come on, we're going to be late," I said.

"I'm not going," he announced.

"What do you mean you're not going?"

"I'm not hungry. I'm going to the gym. Go without me."

I was disappointed, but I didn't make a big show of it. I went down to breakfast alone, and the chef came out and said hello and kept me company for a while. So what if Terry missed one breakfast? We hadn't even gotten to Las Vegas yet, and that's where I had some really good stuff planned.

We had two married friends who lived in Las Vegas, and they were going to take us out to dinner and a show. When we got to our sixteenth-floor suite at the MGM, we found a basket of cheese and fruit and wine waiting for us, and we sat around and had some and marveled at how luxurious the room was. I'm almost ashamed to say what I paid for it, because we couldn't really afford it. But that was why I took a second job—to make our trip extra special. I believed our marriage was worth the expense.

> THERE WERE SO MANY MORE GOOD MOMENTS TO COME, OR SO I THOUGHT.

The evening rolled around, and it was time for us to go downstairs to meet our friends for dinner. But, once again, Terry wasn't bothering to get dressed.

"It's almost time to go," I said.

"I'm not going," he said matter-of-factly.

"Why not?"

"I'm tired."

"Well, can you at least come down and say hello to our friends?" I asked.

"No," he said. "I'm not going anywhere."

I hid my disappointment again and said it was all right, and we could do something together later. I went downstairs alone and told our friends that Terry wasn't feeling well, and as much as I hated doing it I canceled our plans for the night. The dinner and the show. Instead I went to a Subway nearby and picked up two sandwiches for Terry and me. I brought them back to our room and we ate them there. Terry was still moody, so we pretty much sat in silence. But that was okay. I had something big planned for us that night.

"Let's go for a walk," I said after our dinner.

Terry grumbled something, but I pressed him.

"It's a beautiful night," I said. "Come on, we're in Las Vegas."

Reluctantly, Terry came out and we walked together along the main strip. My big surprise was that I'd planned a helicopter ride for us above the bright lights of the strip. I'd never been in a helicopter, and I knew Terry hadn't either. I was so excited I could barely contain myself. But when I told Terry about it, his mood changed for the worse.

"I'm not going," he said. "I'm tired. I'm going back to the room."

I couldn't believe what was happening. The whole situation seemed unreal. I'd spent months making these plans and now they were falling apart. I tried to convince Terry to go on the helicopter ride, but he wasn't having it. All he wanted to do was go back to the room.

We never took that helicopter ride. We trudged back to the MGM in silence, and went to sleep in silence, too. The next morning Terry got up and announced, "I want to go home." We still had two more days in Las Vegas, and then stops in Albuquerque and Memphis, but Terry didn't want to hear about those.

"Let's just get in the car and go," he said. "I want to go home."

I had to call and cancel all our plans. Hotels, dinners, everything. Terry got behind the wheel and he must have driven 80 miles per hour the whole way. We ripped right past Albuquerque without so much as a word. After twelve-straight hours on the road we pulled over and rented a room in a dinky little motel on the highway, just to get some sleep. But at midnight Terry shot up from bed in what looked like a panic.

"Let's go right now," he said. "I want to go home *right now*."

I convinced him to go back to sleep, so we could leave in the morning. Terry got us up at 5:00 a.m. and drove us straight back to Atlanta. The beautiful fourteen-day trip I'd planned turned into eight uncomfortable days. For no reason I could understand Terry had ruined the trip. We argued about it a little, but mostly I was quiet. The anger and disappointment ran so deep I didn't really know how to handle it. And I couldn't figure out why Terry was acting the way he was. Why was he suddenly so tired and grumpy all the time? Why would he rather lay in bed than have fun with me?

There was no big blowout when we got back home. We just went back to the way things were. I tried not to be too angry at Terry for destroying our trip, but a lot of the time I was. And I tried even harder to understand what was going on in his mind, but I wasn't any more successful at that. The disconnect was still there. If anything, we were even further apart.

I let a few weeks pass and then I went back to trying to fix what was broken. I set up marriage counseling for us, first with Apostle Tuff, then with a professional counselor. Those sessions were pretty useless. Terry just sat there and didn't say a word. I mean, not one single word. He let me do all the talking, and he acted like he couldn't be bothered. I just couldn't understand what he was thinking. If there was a serious problem, he wasn't letting me know what it was.

One day after another bad counseling session, Terry and I came home and I went upstairs and he stayed downstairs, as usual. After a while I heard heavy footsteps on the stairs.

Terry stopped in the bedroom doorway. He had his cell phone in his hand, and he had a look on his face I don't think I'd ever seen before. He looked confused and miserable, but also angry and impatient. He just stood there in the doorway for a few moments, saying nothing. I said nothing, too.

And then, finally, he spoke.

"I'm having an affair," he said.

Terry kept talking, but truthfully I didn't hear anything he said after the word *affair*. I just sat there, completely numb. It was like

I blacked out, except I didn't collapse or close my eyes. I just shut down. So many feelings swept through me all at once. Confusion, anger, shame, fear. The familiar gnawing ache of being disgraced, devalued, abandoned. Stray, random moments, like when I took Terry to a clothing store and bought him a new outfit, a nice shirt and a pair of pants and the kind of socks he liked, because he needed new Sunday clothes and I wanted him to have them, and didn't that mean something—wasn't that simple exchange between a man and his wife important? Hadn't it and a thousand moments like it added up to something? The feeling of being less than human, less than deserving, weak and worthless—just like my daddy's step-girls said: *you nothing now and you always gonna be nothing*. The feeling of being inadequate *as a woman*—because what kind of woman allows another woman to walk into her life and just take her husband as she pleases? What kind of woman can't keep her man?

And all of that mixing up into one big, searing ball of pain. Pain like you never felt before.

Because, you see, the moment I heard the word *affair* was the very first time I even *considered* the possibility that Terry was cheating on me.

Now, in an instant, I knew he was. And that realization threw my world into chaos.

/////

The gunman was on a rampage now. He was firing his rifle through the front door, shooting and shooting and not stopping.

Endless explosions were ringing in my ears, and then the sound of more gunshots, these ones coming from outside, and blasting through the entrance doors, shattering the glass, and the gunman kept shooting, and the police kept shooting, and this was the showdown now, the final showdown, the end of it all, the bullets flying so bad, the Devil coming to claim his souls.

For some reason, I did not duck when he fired this time. I did not crouch beneath my desk. Instead I just sat there, calmly watching the gunman shoot. Maybe I was just in shock. But I felt like I had an obligation to watch him, to keep an eye on him and not abandon him in his darkest moment. I know that sounds crazy. I know my only concern should have been the safety of the children, and for sure that was my main concern. And after that I should have been concerned for the teachers, and for the police, and for myself. I should have been praying for one of those bullets to kill the gunman dead.

But I wasn't. I cannot lie. I am just telling you the truth of what was in my head at that moment.

And what was there came from God, because it sure didn't come from me. Even though I was terrified, even though the shooting nearly stopped my heart, even though seeing the gunman shot down was probably the best thing I could have hoped for, that is not what was in my head.

Instead I thought, *This is about saving his soul, too.*

The gunman kept shooting. Glass and shell casings were flying everywhere. I knew if the gunman stayed by the door he would soon be dead. Maybe that was how it had to be. But maybe not. Maybe God had another plan.

"Sweetheart, come back in here," I said, as loud as I could so the gunman could hear me over the shooting. "Bullets don't have no names. And those bullets are gonna kill me and you. I need you to come back in here, and it's gonna be you and me, and we will work this thing out together."

The gunman heard what I said. All of a sudden he stopped shooting. The shooting from outside stopped, too. The gunman kept low and came back into the office and closed the door behind him. He was bleeding from his right elbow, and he was angry because he was bleeding. He was agitated and full of crazy adrenaline. He was out of breath and unstable on his feet. He looked like he was out of control.

But he listened to me. He listened and he stopped shooting and he came back in. I didn't yet know what God's plan was. But I knew it had begun.

///////////////////////////////////////

Let us love one another, for love is of God; and everyone who loves is born of God and knows God. He who does not love does not know God, for God is love.

1 John 4:7–8 NKJV

///////////////////////////////////////

CHAPTER SIX

TUESDAY, AUGUST 20, 2013

Blood ran down the gunman's right forearm in little streams. It didn't look like he'd been shot. Instead it looked like he'd cut himself on the jagged glass of one of the front doors during the shootout. He was wearing a black short-sleeve shirt, so I could clearly see the wound. Then, as soon as he got back in the office with me, his cell phone rang again. This time he didn't answer it. He was too busy being upset with his bleeding. He sat on a chair and took out his water bottle and took a drink.

"I shouldn't have done this," he muttered. "I'm sorry I did this. I know I'm going to die today."

It became my job to convince him otherwise.

His latest shootout with police had rattled me beyond words. It was just so loud and sudden and intense. But I knew that no matter what, I still had to be calm. I couldn't add to his sense of panic by being panicked myself. So everything I said next, I said in a calm and unconcerned voice, as if all the shooting had never happened. As if this was some misbehaving student, not a desperate gunman.

"You're gonna be all right," I said. "God is telling me to tell you you're gonna be all right."

I could see the gunman was barely listening. He was too immersed in his own pain, physical and mental. But I just kept talking.

"God loves you, and so do I," I said. "It's gonna be all right. Do you want me to talk to the police person and tell them everything will be all right?"

The gunman didn't answer. I didn't wait for his say so. I picked up the phone, which already had the dispatcher on the line, and pretended to dial 9-1-1.

"Hello?" I said.

"Yes, ma'am, yes, ma'am," the dispatcher answered, happy to have me back on the call.

"Tell the police to back off," I heard the gunman say.

"He said tell them to back off right now," I said.

"Okay."

"He said tell them to back off," I repeated.

"I don't want the kids," the gunman said. "I want the police. I don't want to hurt the kids."

A wave of relief came over me when he said this. It was the first time he'd even mentioned the children. Maybe it hadn't been his plan all along to come in and shoot the students. Maybe there was no plan at all. Maybe he was just wildly confused. Whatever the case, this was a glimmer of hope.

"He doesn't want the kids," I told the dispatcher. "He wants the police. He wants the police to back off."

The gunman mumbled something I didn't hear.

"What else, sir?" I asked.

"I don't care if I die," he said, almost to himself. "I have nothing to live for and I'm mentally unstable."

He was jumping back and forth between being angry and being resigned. Between wanting to challenge the police, and, it seemed to me, wishing he was dead already. I repeated his words to the dispatcher.

"Okay," she said, "stay on the line with me, okay? Put the phone down if you have to but don't put it on hold so I can't hear."

"Okay," I said.

"Can you tell me where you are?" the dispatcher asked.

"I'm in the front office with him," I said.

Then the angry gunman came back.

"Tell them to send in one of their radios with an unarmed officer," he ordered. "I need some way to talk to the police."

I told the dispatcher what he said.

"If they come in armed, I'm going to start shooting again," he said. "Only one guy."

Then he said something I hadn't expected.

"If they have to, they can go ahead and evacuate them homes across the street," he said. "The ones right in front of the building."

> "IF THEY COME IN ARMED, I'M GOING TO START SHOOTING AGAIN," HE SAID.

For whatever reason, he was concerned that innocent civilians might get caught in his crossfire. He was seeming less and less like someone with nothing but killing on his mind. Still, he had a rifle and plenty of bullets and he was unstable, and worst of all he was ready to die himself. He said he had nothing to live for. He was sure he wouldn't survive the day.

"Is he willing to give his name?" the dispatcher asked me.

I asked the gunman, and he said no.

"If I give my name I'm going to go away for a long, long time," he said. "I'm on probation."

I repeated his words. We heard a small commotion outside the school—a car braking hard or cops running somewhere, just enough racket to pierce the eerie quiet in the office. The gunman flew into a crouch.

"*Tell them to stand down now!*" he screamed.

It was loud enough for the dispatcher to hear. "Tell him I'm giving the police his instructions," she said.

"She said they're giving them instructions," I told him. The gunman shrank back into a posture of resignation.

"I should just shoot myself," he said.

In this moment of extreme despair he must have searched his mind for the name of the one person who cared about him even a little bit—the only one who cared if he lived or died.

"Tell them to call the probation office in DeKalb County," he said. "Let them know what's going on."

I relayed his words.

"Okay, who are we to ask for?" the dispatcher said.

The gunman told me he thought her name was Officer Scott.

"You want me to tell her to come in, sir?" I asked him. "She sounds like she loves you a lot."

This was another ray of hope—a person he trusted, a person who might be able to make him put down his weapon. But the gunman suddenly lost interest in Officer Scott. He drifted back to that dark place of pain and self-pity.

"I should have just went to the hospital instead of doing this," he said. "I'm not on my medication."

I saw an opening.

"I can help you," I said. "You want me to . . . you want me to talk to them? Want me to talk to them and try to—"

"Won't make any difference," he said. "I'm going away for a long time."

"Okay, well let me talk to them and let's see if we can work it out so you don't have to go away with them for a long time."

"It doesn't matter," he said.

"No, it does matter," I said. "I can let them know you have not tried to harm me or do anything with me."

"But I shot at police."

"But that doesn't make any difference. You didn't hit anybody." Then I addressed the police dispatcher.

"Let me ask you this, ma'am," I said. "He didn't hit anybody. He just shot outside the door. If I walk out there with him, they won't shoot him or anything like that, okay?"

The gunman was listening now.

"I want to go to the hospital," he said, almost in a whisper.

"He wants to give himself up," I told the dispatcher. "Is that okay, and they won't shoot him?"

"Yes ma'am," the dispatcher said.

This, it seemed, was God's plan for us. That I would walk out with the gunman, side by side, so that his soul might be spared. His fate and my fate were now intertwined. Yet I knew he was still holding tightly to his rifle, with both hands, ready to shoot again if he had to. He was still the one who held the power of life and death on this day, for himself, and for me, too.

Even so, at that moment, I did not see myself as the gunman's enemy. I knew I had to somehow get him to put his weapon down—until he did, we all still faced death. But I did not view him as a target to be neutralized. You see, by then he was already a person to me. He was one of God's children. Broken and battered, yes, for sure, but still a child of God. I may not have known his name, but I sure knew his *pain*.

In fact, I understand his pain—his fear and his anger and his hopelessness and his sad, pleading wish to just *cease to be*—better than he could have ever known.

If I didn't have to get up at 5:00 a.m. to take care of Derrick, I would still have to get up at 5:00 a.m. to take care of his daddy.

My husband and I had a morning ritual that looked a lot like the one I had with my son. Mainly, it involved me taking care of him. That was me—I was the caregiver. Up in the darkness, say a few prayers, read my Bible at the kitchen table for a bit, then fire up the stove and get working on his breakfast. Oatmeal, fresh fruit, a banana for the potassium, some orange juice, and a cup of special tea that he likes. While he's eating breakfast I get started

This, it seemed, was God's plan for us. That I would walk out with the gunman, side by side, so that his soul might be spared. His fate and my fate were now intertwined.

on his lunch and dinner. Sauté some fish and some brown rice, a vegetable or two, then something different for dinner—baked chicken, sweet potatoes, some kind of green. If he is working I put his lunch and dinner in bowls so he can take them with him and have them there, and I pack his lunch pail with little snack bags, organic nuts, berries, banana chips, trail mix, stuff like that, and maybe some all-natural popcorn with this special seasoning he loves, as a treat now and then.

I get all of that done by 6:15, plus my son's breakfast and lunch and dinner, so I can run upstairs and get myself ready and be at work by 7:00 a.m. I work my two or three jobs and I'm back home at 7:00 p.m., and if Terry is working late I might run his dinner over to him at his job, so it'll be fresher and so he can eat it right in the car while I drive him back home, because I know how hungry he is.

Every night when the kids were young the four of us ate dinner together at the table. There was rarely any reason for us to ever miss our supper together. My momma had taught me how to cook, and my mother-in-law, too, and I learned a lot of recipes on my own. One year I even talked to a nutritionist because Terry's cholesterol was really high and he weighed around 230 pounds. I had to get his cholesterol numbers down from 215 to 150, and his weight down to below 200, both of which I did, though it was hard work getting Terry to eat right.

Then one day Terry passed out at work and I took him to see the doctor, and the doctor hooked him up to a heart monitor and we learned that Terry's heart was stopping nearly every three minutes, and if we didn't do something about it Terry was surely going to have a heart attack. So Terry had emergency heart surgery, and the doctors implanted a pacemaker, and I was right by Terry's side for every doctor visit, his whole hospital stay, and the months afterward when he needed special care.

And then his feet started to hurt, so bad he could hardly walk sometimes, and we had a plan to start our own private transportation company by then, and Terry is working for a bus outfit, Southeastern Stages, and he's learning the business as he goes, and we set aside some money so we can go to a mobile coach conference, where we can network and make contacts and get our business going, but instead Terry tells me he wants to fix his feet. And as much as I hate to do it—as much as I don't want to delay our plans for the future—we use the money for the conference to get Terry an operation to fix his feet. And after the operation he has to stay off his feet for weeks and weeks, and so I take care of him at home, in between my own work shifts, cooking him meals, bringing him his meals, washing his dishes once he finished his meals—tending to him so he can get better and we can get on with our future.

I did all of these things because that is what a wife does, what a mother does, what a woman does—she makes a family work. She takes care of her man. Like the Bible says, "The heart of her husband trusts in her, and he will have no lack of gain. She does him good, and not harm, all the days of her life."

The truth is, I was more than happy to do all these things. Get up in the darkness every single day, feed my family before I took a single bite myself, put my last dollar into fixing my husband's feet, use up all my work insurance on him so that my own medical bills got sent back to me—whatever was needed I did without question, and with nothing but love. I treasured my family more than anything else besides God, and I knew no life other than the one that had my family in it. I never wanted any other life but that.

And so, on that awful day when I learned the very foundation of my life was crumbling beneath me, I think you'll understand when I say I didn't take it well.

/////

If Terry told me any of the details of his affair after admitting to it in our bedroom, I did not hear them and I didn't care to. Once my shock subsided and my numbness went away, all I cared about was fixing what was broken. There was no Plan B. There was only a plan to save our marriage. No other possibility made the slightest bit of sense. If Terry didn't love me anymore, I just had to find a way to make him love me again.

A few days after his admission we went back to marriage counseling. I set up a session with a new therapist who worked out of an office in Stone Mountain, Georgia. In our first meeting with this therapist, a middle-aged man with a reassuring demeanor, I spoke first. I explained what happened, and talked a little about our marriage, and said we were both determined to heal this wound and go back to being a family. Terry didn't say a word. Silent the whole fifty minutes. We went home and he was silent some more.

At the next session, Terry kept his mouth closed again, until the therapist finally turned to him and said, "Terry, you have to talk. You have to be honest. You have to look at your wife and be completely honest and tell her everything that is happening, or else this is not going to work."

Like I said, up until that point I knew few details of Terry's affair. I certainly didn't know why he had strayed, or how long it had been going on. To me, these didn't seem like the most important details, or at least not as important as what we could do to put it all behind us.

Yet Terry listened to the counselor, and the truth came out. All of it.

"I have been with this other lady for a long while now," was the first thing I recall him saying. "Since before January."

January was months earlier. January was when he was laid up in bed and I was tending to him after his foot operation. January! I swear I could feel my heart stop beating when he said these words. But the truth was only starting to come. There was plenty more.

"It was a sexual thing," Terry said. "She does things for me that she"—pointing to me—"won't do."

Then he described those things.

I was shattered. Oh, God, was I shattered. I had no idea this was coming. He'd never talked to me about any of it, never complained about anything, so all of it was a total shock. Sitting on the sofa next to my husband, I felt my body start to shake. I had no control over my own nerves. I tried to draw a breath but it got stuck somewhere in my chest. I teetered forward, then backward. I blinked my eyes a few times, like I was just waking up and didn't know where I was. I tried to breathe again and still couldn't. A thought formed: *You are having an anxiety attack.*

"Are you okay?" the therapist asked, looking at me with fatherly concern.

"I'm okay," I said, trying to sound defiant, though clearly I wasn't either okay or defiant.

"He has to keep going," the therapist told me. "He needs to get all this out."

Oh, I thought, *that's well and good, but what about what I need?*

Terry kept talking. He mentioned other things he liked about this woman, and he talked about other things they had done together. I started doing the math in my head. I thought back to our ruined road trip and realized Terry was probably thinking about another woman by then. That's why he didn't want to do anything with me, and that's why he couldn't wait to get back home. I thought of all the time he spent downstairs by himself, and all the phone calls he must have been making to her behind my back. I thought of the two of them together—happy, laughing, doing things I wouldn't do—and I felt like I might throw up right there in the therapist's office. This was more shocking than when Terry told me about the affair, because then I had no idea how serious it was. But now, I knew it all. Terry just kept talking, just kept "being honest." He was bringing this other woman to life right in front of me. He spoke about her in an intimate, affectionate way, like she was his wife and I was someone else, and that's when a horrible, staggering realization hit me.

This is not going to be okay.

We left the therapist's office and got in the car and Terry pulled out into traffic. I sat next to him and felt a strange sensation—the sensation of life draining out of me. All my strength and will and resolve was gone, leaving only the shell of a person slumped in the passenger seat. It was like the Devil just came and sucked the life right out of me, because that is what the enemy does, he comes to steal and kill and destroy, and now he had stolen and killed and destroyed my marriage, and in the process he was destroying me. I began to let out huge, loud wails, and Terry turned to me and said meekly, "It's going to be okay."

"It's not . . . going . . . to be . . . okay," I said, barely spitting out the words between sobs. I felt like I had no control over my emotions, or my brain, or even my physical body. I just sat there, my chest heaving, tears and spit all over my face, limp and lifeless, completely inconsolable. Maybe I had never truly considered a life without Terry until this very moment. Maybe that's why I was so out-of-control.

"I'M OKAY," I SAID, TRYING TO SOUND DEFIANT, THOUGH CLEARLY I WASN'T EITHER OKAY OR DEFIANT.

Without even thinking about it, my left hand reached for the handle of the passenger door.

The car was rolling at 40 miles per hour. I tried to open the door but it was locked. I fumbled to unlock it, sobbing and shaking my head back and forth. I got the door open a crack. Terry reached over and grabbed me by the arm, hard.

"What are you doing, baby??"

I had the urge to throw the door open and heave myself into traffic. Now, I do not know if I would have actually done it. But if

I am being honest, I did have the urge to do it. It would have been an act of relief, of getting away, of escaping the unbearable pain, of somehow setting myself free. This seemed like the best and easiest way to do it, and the only way available at that moment. I leaned toward the open door. Terry held tightly to my arm and pulled me back toward him while he kept steering.

"What are you doing?" he cried. "It's going to be okay."

"It's not going to be okay," I said for a second time. And even then, even in all that confusion and torment, I knew that this was true.

/////

Terry pulled the car over to give me a chance to calm down. But I just couldn't. He called his aunt, who lived nearby, and we drove there so she could talk to me. When we pulled into her driveway I got out of the car and tried to stand up, but my legs didn't work. I collapsed in a pile right there on the asphalt. Terry and his uncle picked me up and got me inside and put me on the sofa, but I was crying so hard I rolled right off the sofa, so now I was a pile on the living room floor. I had never felt so out of control in my life. I was like a three-year-old girl who can't stop crying and ends up swallowing every breath. I just wanted my brain to stop working, so I could disappear into darkness. I wanted to slip into the deepest sleep and have someone wake me up in a year. I wanted to *cease to be*.

But the thing is, you can't hide from betrayal. You can't outrun sorrow. You can't close your eyes and expect pain to go away.

These things stay with you, seep into your bones and tissue—they *become* you. You have no choice but to let them have away at you.

I could hear Terry's voice in between my sobs. He kept saying "I'm sorry" over and over again. I heard his uncle talk to him and say, "Terry, this ain't right. You have to break it off with this woman." I heard Terry reply, "Okay, I'll break it off." His words didn't mean much to me as I lay on the floor of his aunt's house, but over the next few days they did. At least he was willing to try and fix what was broken. Maybe I hadn't lost him yet.

Terry agreed to stay in marriage counseling and to regularly visit with his uncle, who became his mentor. At home things were awkward, with a lot of long silences. All the hurt and anger and sadness was still there. But from what I could tell we were both trying to get past what had happened. I didn't expect us to go back to normal overnight.

Terry never spoke about the other woman to me, and after a few days I started wondering if he'd actually broken it off with her. One day when we were out for drive I asked him point-blank if he had.

"Yes I did," he said.

"Well, if you did, then get your phone out and call her right now and tell her again it's over," I said.

Terry got out his phone and made a call.

"Hello?" he said. "Yeah, it's me. I just want to make sure you're clear on this, that I can't see you no more."

She said something I couldn't hear, and then Terry said, "Yeah," and then he looked at me as if to ask, "Is this what you wanted to hear?"

"Let me talk to her," I said.

Terry handed me the phone.

"Listen here," I said. "Me and Terry are trying to work out our marriage. You leave him alone and leave us to our lives."

The woman on the other end was quiet for a while, before saying, "Okay."

"You and Terry are over, you understand that?"

"Yes I do,' she said.

"Good," I said. Then I handed the phone back to Terry, and he hung up.

"That's done and over with then," I said.

For the first time in days I felt a little bit of hope. This wasn't going to be easy, but whatever it took to put our marriage back together, we were going to do it.

Over the new week or so, however, Terry went back to acting cold and distant. He lingered downstairs for hours, same as before. One day I noticed him punching a code into his phone. He'd never used a security code to open his cell phone before, and now suddenly he was. I began to wonder if he really had broken off his affair.

I went to the website of our phone provider and looked at all our calls. I sat at the kitchen table and went down the list, looking for numbers I didn't recognize. I found one, then another, and another, and dozens more. My heart was racing so fast I could hear it thumping through my chest. I took a deep breath and got out my cell and called the first number I didn't know.

In the course of the next two hours I learned my husband had not just cheated on me with one woman. He had cheated on me with *three* women.

What's more, the woman he called on his cell right in front of me wasn't even his most current fling. It was one of his older affairs, and he apparently had called her two days earlier to say he might need her to pretend to be someone else. She went along with it, and—just that easily—Terry convinced me the affair was over.

But it wasn't. Nor was our marriage beginning to heal. In fact, the pain and desolation were only just beginning.

/////

I confronted Terry about the other affairs and he confessed to them all. But he wasn't apologetic in the least. If anything he was defiant. When I asked him how he could stand before God in light of all his sins, he quickly brushed me off. "I know what I'm doing is wrong and I know God would not approve, and I will have to be accountable for it, but so be it," I recall him saying. "Because right now this is where I'm at."

Before long Terry told me he was moving out. I didn't protest, because I believed some time apart could help. I figured if I gave Terry space he might come to his senses. I still believed with all my heart our marriage could be saved. On some days Terry gave me hope. He'd come around and be softer and more vulnerable than usual, and he would even talk about the terrible mistake he'd made by cheating on me. He would talk about the other woman and say she was no good for him. I found myself consoling him, and telling him everything would be just fine. Those nights together gave me hope.

But then, on a dime, Terry would go back to being distant and secretive. One minute he'd tell me he and this other woman were finished, and the next it was obvious they weren't. I finally decided I had to find out for myself where I stood. I had to see him and this other woman together.

One morning I called the dispatcher at my husband's work to find out if he was coming in that day. I told the dispatcher, a friend of ours, that we were having problems and I needed to see Terry. Suddenly, the dispatcher started crying.

"I don't want to get involved," he said. "But I'm so sorry for what's going on."

That is when I realized things were much worse than I thought.

I drove to my husband's job and waited across the street from the bus depot to watch him pull up. Finally he arrived and pulled his car up to the front entrance. I watched him slowly get out of the driver's seat. Then I saw the passenger door open, and a woman step out. She was in her early forties, like me, and maybe a little darker-skinned. She walked around the front of the car and went straight to Terry.

Then he hugged her and kissed her and patted her behind like she was his wife.

They were intimate and familiar in a way Terry and I had long stopped being. I had been replaced. This woman had taken over for me in every way—physically, emotionally, spiritually. The shock of seeing that is almost indescribable. No wife should ever have to see that. That lonely moment I sat in my car, crouching and hiding like a thief and watching my worst fears realized, is a moment I wouldn't wish on anyone. It was a moment that stripped me of my humanity and left me naked. Everything that came before, all the cooking and cleaning and the trips and adventures and the births of our children and the dinners together and the love that we shared and the life that we built—none of it mattered anymore. It was all just junk, just garbage. Disposable, worthless, adding up to nothing. Already gone.

I squeezed the steering wheel and I watched Terry hug this woman and I felt like this day wasn't happening—like it couldn't be happening. My Terry? The Terry I knew? He would never allow some woman to steal and kill and destroy what we had. He would never allow anyone to just walk in and so casually wreck our world. Terry was my protector, and I was his, and that's the way it had been for thirty-three years. So this could not be happening. It just didn't make any sense.

But, of course, he wasn't my Terry anymore.

///////

I watched the woman get back in Terry's car and drive away, like wives do. Suddenly I felt very angry. Extremely angry. *Enraged*. I pulled out of my hiding spot and drove through the gates of the bus depot and parked right where Terry's car had been, next to the main entrance. I told the dispatcher to tell Terry I was there.

At first Terry refused to come out. Finally, he did. "No more lies," I told him. "I have seen the truth with my own eyes now. You cannot deceive me anymore. So please, please just tell me the truth. For once just tell me the truth."

"It's not like that," Terry insisted.

"I saw you!" I said, tears running down my face now. "I saw you hug her and kiss her like she's your wife!"

"It's not like that," he repeated.

"Is she living with you? No more lies!"

"No, she just came down for a visit. She lives in South Carolina."

I didn't know what to believe anymore. I was hurt and tired and in shock.

"Okay," I finally said, "you win. I give up. I am through with all this."

"Marie, please . . ."

"I can't take it anymore," I said. "I just can't take it anymore."

I got back in my car and drove away and went to work and tried to banish Terry from my mind, but I couldn't. And over the next few weeks he didn't make it any easier on me. He kept coming around and dropping hints he might want to reconcile. He kept throwing me a lifeline. And, though I know I shouldn't have, I grabbed it and I held on hard. My life was an endless bobbing wave, dragging me under, spitting me back out, denying me breath then giving it to me, mixing little bursts of sunlight with silent darkness. But little bursts were all I needed.

And so I kept trying to make our marriage work.

Three weeks later Terry reneged on a promise to come see me on our wedding anniversary. It was the first wedding anniversary we ever spent apart. When my birthday rolled around he promised to come see, but once again he didn't show.

"I'm not coming," he said when I called him. "Get over it."

I soon learned he spent both those days with the other woman.

He came by another day to claim some of his things. I cried as I watched him pack a few bags and boxes. I drew the line when he wanted to take the nicer of our two vacuum cleaners.

My life was an endless bobbing wave, dragging me under, spitting me back out, denying me breath then giving it to me.

"No," I said. "You'll have the raggedy one."

He also wanted to take one of our children's beds, but I said no to that, too.

Then he was gone.

I would later learn he cashed in his 401(k) to rent a new Lincoln Navigator for him and the other woman. He used the rest of the money to rent a new townhouse in an Atlanta neighborhood, where he lived with the other woman and her daughter.

At some point during the whole ordeal Terry pawned his wedding ring. I don't know what he used that money for.

I felt so sick and miserable I finally dragged myself to see a doctor. The doctor put me through a bunch of tests and told me I was on my way to killing myself with stress. I went to see a psychiatrist, who put me on antidepressants for the first time in my life. I was doing everything I could to stay afloat, but it wasn't easy. I prayed and prayed to God for any help or direction He could give me, but I didn't see any. Nothing I was doing was working. Nothing could lift the blackness. No one—not even God—could make me feel like my life was worth a nickel.

Unless you have been abandoned you can't understand what a deep and terrible wound it can be. It is enough to make you want to stop living.

One chilly November afternoon I drove to a shopping center in Decatur, about seven miles east of Atlanta, and parked along Wesley Chapel Road. The road was a three-lane stretch that was always busy right after work. I sat in my car and watched the Fords and Chevys and SUVs barrel past, people rushing home to be with their children and their partners, anxious to get back to their real lives. As for me, I had no life without Terry. Or at least that's what I believed with all my heart.

I opened the door and got out of the car. I walked to the side of Wesley Chapel Road and stood there. I was only three or four paces from the traffic. I was tired of all the lies and all the back and forth and all the desperation to make Terry love me, and I just wanted all of it to end. I no longer believed this was something I could fix. That little lifeline I was clinging to had long since slipped out of my hands.

I took one step forward. Then another. All I'd have to do is take another two steps, and it would all be over. That was it—just two simple steps. I watched the headlights rush toward me, blinding me to the world.

And I prayed and I cried and I thought, *God, forgive me.*

///////////////////////////////////////

To every thing there is a season,
and a time to every purpose
under the heaven. . . . A time
to cast away stones, and a time
to gather stones together;
a time to embrace, and a time
to refrain from embracing.

Ecclesiastes 3:1, 5

///////////////////////////////////////

CHAPTER SEVEN

There on the side of Wesley Chapel Road, with cars speeding by so close I could feel them, I thought about my children. I thought about what their faces would look like when they found out I was dead. Who would be the one to tell them? Who would sit with them while they cried? I love my children more than I can possibly describe, but still, I was standing by the road, inches from death, ready to leave them without a mother. Suddenly I felt deeply ashamed. Some drivers honked, as if to warn me I was too close to the road. I took a step back, took out my cell phone, and called Terry.

I told him where I was and what I was thinking of doing.

"Don't do it," he said. "Step back from the road. Get back in your car. Marie, listen to me. *Get back in the car and talk to me.*"

I turned around and slowly walked back to my car, like I was in a trance. In between sobs I heard Terry tell me I was stronger than I knew. But was I? All I could think in those moments was, *I don't know how to live without this man. I don't know what to do next.* Where was this strength he was talking about? Where was it when I nearly left my children motherless?

Terry talked to me for a while, until I calmed down a bit. He told me I should drive to our church, and he would call ahead and tell them I was coming and what was going on. I drove to the church and two ladies who worked there greeted me at the door. I went in and screamed and cried and they held me and prayed with me and told me everything would be all right. After that I drove home and got into my bed and tried to sleep. And I did sleep, fitfully, an hour or two, and then the sun came up and it was a new day and I was still alive.

> I SUSPECTED IT WAS NOT GOD'S WISH FOR ME TO PERISH JUST YET.

That I was able to greet another day was, in my mind, a miracle, an act of God. I suspected it was not God's wish for me to perish just yet. He had some other plan for me; I just didn't know what it was. We all have a purpose on this earth, and while that purpose isn't always ours to know, we must be ready when the time comes, so we can serve the Lord as He sees fit. That is why God walked me back from the side of the road, one slow step at a time. Because He had some other purpose for me.

Still, I couldn't hide from the awful truth of what I had done. I couldn't deny that, on that day, I was ready to die.

/////

The gunman was bleeding, and the blood seemed to surprise him. He looked at his forearm and touched the blood and slumped in a chair, almost like a child. Some of the anger seemed to go out of him then. It was as if the blood had weakened his resolve. For a moment he looked like someone who knew he was defeated—not just that day, but in life. Yet he still had the rifle slung around his shoulder, and he still had all the power. The demon inside him would have his chance at victory as long as the shooter had his gun.

By then, however, I understood I had a weapon I could use to push back at the enemy. It was the only weapon I had, but, in this situation, it was a good one. It was a simple and common thing, something that is part of our lives each and every day, or at least ought to be. It is something God commands us to show.

My weapon was compassion.

"To the weak became I as weak, that I might gain the weak," it says in 1 Corinthians 9:22. "I am made all things to all men, that I might by all means save some."

Think of the power of those words! To help the weak, our Lord *became as weak*—He walked in their shoes and felt what they felt and loved them at their very worst. The strongest and most powerful, walking among the weakest and most frail! The God-fearing among us deal gently with "those who are ignorant and [are] going astray," it says in Hebrews 5:2, "since he himself is also subject to weakness" (NKJV). Well, I was subject to weakness—Lord knows I was subject to weakness. It was not too hard for me to put myself in the gunman's shoes. So it fell to me to become as weak so I might gain the weak.

It fell to me to show compassion to the gunman.

I got back on the phone with the 9-1-1 dispatcher.

"If I walk out there with him," I asked her, "they won't shoot him or anything like that, okay? He wants to give himself up. Is that okay, and they won't shoot him?"

141

"Yes ma'am," the dispatcher said. "Hold on one moment."

I told the gunman the dispatcher was talking to the police and working things out so he could give himself up.

"And I'll go out there with you," I assured him.

The gunman's shoulders were slumped and his body was listless. He wasn't pacing anymore. He seemed far away. He looked like he could no longer handle the pain and torment he felt. Whatever fury he came in with seemed gone now.

"I feel so bad about my life," he said softly.

"Well, don't feel bad, baby," I said. "My husband just left me after thirty-three years."

"But I don't even have anyone."

"But yes you do," I said. "I'm sitting here with you and talking to you about it. I also got a son that's multiple disabled. Let me talk to her and let her know that I'm going out with you. You want me to talk to her?"

"This has to end bad," he said.

"No it doesn't, baby," I said. "This is all going to be well. The lady is going to talk to the police, okay? Just hold on a second."

I got back on with the dispatcher and tried to hurry things along. I couldn't be sure the gunman was even listening to what I was saying. I figured he was in too much pain—not physical, but emotional and mental—to be able to think straight. I understood that. I knew what it was like to walk right up to the line between sanity and madness, and be ready to walk across it. The gunman was right at the line. He could still go either way.

"Go on the intercom and tell everyone I'm sorry," he said suddenly.

"Hold on," I told the dispatcher. "He wants me to go over to the intercom."

"Apologize for what I did today," he said. "Tell them I never wanted to hurt any kids."

I put down the receiver and picked up the intercom microphone and switched it on.

"This is a message from the intruder," I said, hoping there wasn't anyone left in the school to hear me. "He wants to say he's sorry for what he done. He didn't mean to do it, and he never wanted to hurt any kids. He just wants to apologize, okay. So this is him saying he's sorry."

I switched off the intercom. Then the gunman and I were quiet for a while.

///////

I think I probably had four or five suicidal moments in all.

Some were worse than others; not all of them brought me to the side of a road. But they were all terrible moments when I believed with all my heart that the only escape from the pain I felt was to end my life. I went to see doctors and psychologists and counsel ors, and I went to church and prayed and talked to Apostle, and I listened when my friends and family gave me advice and told me everything would be okay, and I truly did all of these things. I tried everything I could to not feel the way I felt.

But there were times when I just couldn't help it. There were times I felt I had no other way out.

I KNEW WHAT IT WAS
LIKE TO WALK RIGHT UP
TO THE LINE BETWEEN
SANITY AND MADNESS,
AND BE READY TO
WALK ACROSS IT. THE
GUNMAN WAS RIGHT AT
THE LINE: HE COULD
STILL GO EITHER WAY.

After the incident on Wesley Chapel Road, I tried hard to convince myself that Terry didn't love me anymore. Maybe that should have been obvious to me by then, but it wasn't. Terry was a lingering presence in my life, and as long as he kept coming around, I was able to cling to even the slightest bit of hope that I could make him love me again.

"She ain't no good for me," he would tell me one day. And the next, "Move on with your life." This had been the pattern for months—pulling back in, pushing away.

I wish I could say I stopped letting Terry string me along like this, but I can't say that. I can't say that at all. Every time I was in his presence, all my resolve melted away.

But I had to stop kidding myself. I had to stop trying to make Terry love me again, and I had to stop saying things to try and win him back. I could no longer fight this battle on my own. I had to hand it over to God and let Him fight it for me.

With the help of a friend I drew up separation papers. That was the first step toward Terry and me dissolving our marriage once and for all. It was not an easy step, that's for sure. It felt like I was taking the only man I ever loved, and the last thirty-three years of my life, and any future chance I'd ever have at happiness, and stuffing them in a trash bag and throwing them to the curb. Doing all that was impossibly sad. But it was something I had to do.

I asked Terry to come over and sign the separation papers. On the phone he said he would, but as he sat on the sofa, he let out a huge sigh.

"I don't know what I'm doing," he said. "She's no good for me."

I sat next to him and realized how much I missed him. It occurred to me I could forgive Terry for everything he had done—the
affairs, the lies, the manipulation, everything. I had it in my heart
to forgive all that, and to love him as much as ever. All Terry had
to do to make that happen was come back home to me.

I leaned in and tried to give him a hug.

Terry pushed me away.

"That ain't fair to her," he said.

I recoiled in shock. I shouldn't have been shocked, but I was. I
was his wife, and this wasn't fair to *her*?

"What about me?" I pleaded. "I need you here, with me. What
about what's fair to me??"

Terry stood up and looked at me. He might as well have been
looking at a customer on one of the buses he drove.

"She's not as strong as you," he said matter-of-factly. "You will
survive, she wouldn't. You're strong, you'll get over this."

Then he left without signing the papers. I sat there as the familiar blackness came down on my head. My torment wasn't over. I
hadn't found a way out of it yet.

/////

I couldn't be sure, but I felt like the apology over the intercom
brought the gunman some small measure of peace. I hoped it was
the event that turned the tide. Maybe he realized his best way out
of this mess was not to shoot and kill and destroy, but to surrender.
There is always another option. It's just that sometimes we're too
distressed to see it.

"What do they want me to do with the gun?" he said after a while. My heart leapt when he said it.

I got back on the phone with the dispatcher.

"Okay, he's going to come out now, but he wants to know, what do you want him to do with the gun?"

"Or I could lay on the floor with my hands behind my back," the gunman said. He was cooperating now.

"Or do you want to send a police officer in, and he said he'll be on the ground with his hands behind his back?" I asked the dispatcher. "I'll take the gun from him and put it on the other side over by me."

"Okay, one moment," the dispatcher said.

The gunman was facing me but his head was down and he still wasn't making eye contact. And the AK-47 was still strapped around him.

> I SAT THERE AS THE FAMILIAR BLACKNESS CAME DOWN ON MY HEAD. My TORMENT WASN'T OVER.

"Why don't you take the gun and put it over here on the counter," I said.

"Okay," he answered meekly.

He took hold of the strap and pulled it over his head and walked to the counter and gently laid the AK-47 down. Then he walked back and got his book bag.

"Here, put that over here," I told him, pointing to another section of the counter. He walked over and put the book bag there.

Then he reached into his pockets and took out all the stray bullets. He put them on the counter and pushed them together so they wouldn't roll off.

"He's put his weapons down?" the dispatcher asked me.

"Yes, but hold on before you come in," I said. "He's putting everything down. He's going to get on the floor so tell them to hold on a minute. Let him get everything together. He's getting it all together."

The gunman went to the middle of the room, got down on his knees and lowered himself to the floor, face down. Then he put his hands together behind his back.

"Okay," I said to him, "tell me when you're ready and I'll tell them to come in."

"I need a drink of water," he said.

"He wants to drink his bottle of water," I told the dispatcher. "Let him get it together."

The gunman got off the floor, went to his book bag, and took a long drink out of his bottle. Then he put the bottle back and lay back down on the floor. When he was settled there, he quietly said, "Everyone is going to hate me."

I knew this was a dangerous person who had stormed a school with an AK-47 and terrorized hundreds of children and quite possibly intended to kill as many people as he could, including me. But even so, at that moment, I felt sorry for him.

"We're not going to hate you, baby," I said. "It's a good thing you've given up. We're not going to hate you. So let's just do it before the helicopters and stuff like that come."

"Tell them the gun may come back stolen but it's not," he said. "I know the story behind it and I will tell them all that."

I relayed his message.

"Do they want me to take my belt off?" he said.

I asked the dispatcher. "She said that's fine, just take all your weapons off," I told him.

"I got no more weapons," he said.

"He's on the ground now with his hands behind his back," I told the dispatcher. "Tell the officers don't come in shooting or anything. They can come on in and I'll buzz them in."

"Okay," the dispatcher said.

For the next few minutes there was nothing but silence. I imagined the police were figuring out how to come in and get him. They couldn't be sure his weapons were down. They had to assume this could be a trap. So while they planned their strategy, the gunman and I waited. I heard a distant siren and what I thought sounded like a helicopter, but for the most part the office was eerily quiet. I sat at my desk. The gunman lay on the floor, hands behind his back. His weapon and ammunition were on the counter three feet away. Not for a moment did I think to reach for the rifle. I wouldn't have known what to do with it if I got it. My job was to keep the gunman calm until the police came in.

> WHEN HE WAS SETTLED THERE, HE QUIETLY SAID, "EVERYONE IS GOING TO HATE ME."

But as he lay on the ground I could tell he was getting agitated again. Things were taking too long.

"Where are they?" he said, making a move to get up.

"Hold on, just stay right there," I said. "I'll buzz them in so you'll know when they're coming, okay?" I said.

"They're going to shoot me."

"Don't worry about it, I'll sit right here so they'll see you didn't try to harm me, okay?"

"I don't know," the gunman said, pulling himself up into a sitting position. The rifle was nearly within his arm's reach. "I really messed up," he said. "Where are they? What are they going to do?"

"It's going to be all right, sweetie," I said as calmly as I could. "I just want you to know I love you, okay, and I am proud of you. That's a good thing you've given up, and don't worry about it. We all go through something in life."

The gunman got quiet. I couldn't tell if he was angry or resigned. I was afraid he'd jump up and grab his rifle again. It was right there for him to pick up. I had no idea what would happen next.

"I just want to die," the gunman said.

Those words struck a chord with me because, not all that long ago, I had said them myself.

"No, you don't want that," I told him. "You're going to be okay. I thought the same thing. You know, I tried to commit suicide last year after my husband left me, but look at me now. I'm still working and everything is okay."

The gunman got quiet again. He was facing me, but he still wasn't looking at me. It was almost as if he couldn't bear to make eye contact with anyone, so no one could see just how much pain he was in, or just how inhuman he felt. So he looked down at the floor instead. But I knew he was listening to me. I knew I was getting through.

Then the gunman said something remarkable.

"Do you remember me?" he said. "My name is Michael Hill."

//

Have mercy on me, O Lord, for
I am weak; O Lord, heal me,
for my bones are troubled.

Psalm 6:2 NKJV

//

CHAPTER EIGHT

Michael Brandon Hill—his family called him Brandon—
grew up just like most kids, or at least that's what his
older brother Timothy told Piers Morgan on CNN. For the first
thirteen years of his life there was no indication Michael had anything seriously wrong with him. He and Tim played tag together,
threw footballs, romped in the woods, and just did "kidly stuff."
But when Michael turned thirteen he started "having problems,"
his brother said. "He had his good times, and he had his bad
times."

Like my son, Derrick, Michael apparently suffered from attention deficit disorder. I'm sure that led him to act out and get
tagged as a troublemaker. That's what happened with my son. But,
according to his brother, Michael had more serious problems than
ADD—he was also bipolar. He may have also been schizophrenic.
He had to take so many pills for his disorders his brother said their
house looked like a drugstore.

When he was fifteen Michael Hill was arrested for burglary.
In his mug shot he doesn't look that much different from when I
met him. At that point in his life, it seems, Michael went off the
rails. One night his family woke up to the smell of smoke, and

Tim discovered someone had started a fire in the attic. The eight people in the house got out safely, and only later did they learn it was Michael who set the fire.

Another night his mother was asleep in her bed and heard a sound. She opened her eyes and saw Michael standing over her, holding a butcher knife. After that his mother collected every last knife in the house and kept them locked in the trunk of her car.

Michael saw many different doctors, who put him on many different pills. It was not like people ignored his problems; his family and those around him apparently did everything they could to get Michael the help he needed. In fact, he was institutionalized somewhere around ten times, usually involuntarily, so doctors could try different treatments. Sometimes a new medication worked for a while, but Michael always seemed to slip back to being erratic and unpredictable. He wasn't violent all the time, but he could "turn on a dime," Tim said.

According to Tim, Michael tried to kill himself "too many times to count."

Then came December 31, 2012.

That night, Michael and his brother got into some kind of fight. It seems Michael posted some threats on Facebook—something like he was going to shoot Tim in the head and not think twice about it. Tim, fearing for his life, called the police. Authorities got ahold of Michael before anything bad happened, and the next spring he pled guilty to making terroristic threats. He got three years probation and mandatory anger management treatments. He was also ordered to stay away from his brother.

It looks like Michael didn't have much contact with his family after that. For a while he lived with a Georgia pastor and his wife, who later told reporters that Michael was quiet and never acted violently. In 2013 he lived with a couple and three or four other people in a house on East Lilac Lane in Decatur, within walking distance of McNair Academy. One of his neighbors said he often saw Michael babysitting three children, and called him "just an average guy." If Michael was slipping deeper and deeper into his own darkness in those months, it seems he did a pretty good job of hiding it. The pastor's wife told a reporter that Michael's Medicaid recently expired, forcing him to go off his medication. "He didn't really let anyone know," she said.

But it's clear from what wound up happening that Michael was, in fact, suffering greatly in the weeks before August 20, 2013. We may never know just how hopeless and despairing Michael got, and we may never find out why he felt there was only one thing he could do to ease his pain.

What we do know is that in the days before August 20, Michael Hill got his hands on an AK-47. On the morning of August 20 he got up and took a cell phone photo of himself holding the rifle—a final portrait, he might have thought. Not long after that he got in a car and drove the short distance to McNair Academy. He waited for someone to pass through the locked front door and then he snuck inside.

The whole thing was a desperate, desperate cry for help, the pastor's wife told reporters. "Unfortunately, he didn't know a better way to get it."

/////

All the back-and-forth with Terry and me finally came to a head on New Year's Eve 2012.

We'd made plans to get together that evening and talk some more about what needed to happen next for us. I was trying to get him to sign separation papers, and ultimately divorce papers, but at the same time, way deep down, I was still trying to win him back. Every opportunity to be with Terry face-to-face was another opportunity to turn things around. New Year's Eve was another chance to make him see the error of his ways.

I waited at home for Terry to show up, but, not surprisingly, he never did. I called him on the phone and he picked up. I asked him where he was and why he wasn't here yet. That's when Terry tore into me with a vengeance.

"This is all your fault," he said. "This whole thing is your fault. I don't know how many times I have to tell you, but I am going to be with her. I don't want you, I want to be with her. So get on with your life because *I don't want you anymore.*"

Then he hung up.

Terry had never spoken to me this way, ever. Even in our worst moments he hadn't been this harsh. It looked like he always tried to be a little careful with my feelings. But this time he talked to me like I was someone he didn't respect in the least. Like I was some stranger he had to shake off his tail, or someone he hated and never wanted to see again. Was that who I was to him? Already part of his past? And had this been all my fault? Did I deserve to be treated this way?

I was hurt and confused and angry. I got in my car and drove to

Terry's apartment. When I got there all the lights were off and his car was gone. He hadn't even been home, hadn't ever planned to see me. He was away somewhere celebrating New Year's Eve with her. I turned my car around and drove to the home of a friend I knew from church. I parked on the street outside his home and called him on my cell. I was all out of options and all done with trying. I had no one to turn to and nowhere to go. I felt completely stripped of dignity and something less than human. It was just me buried beneath a mountain of pain, and I only had one way out.

"Hello?" my friend said.

"It's Antoinette," I said. "Can you help me get a gun?"

I cannot say for sure what I would have done if I ever got my hands on a weapon. Do I believe I might have ended my life? I certainly felt bad enough at that moment to do it. Who can say what we're capable of when we're pushed past what we can endure.

"Slow down," my friend said to me on the phone. "Tell me what's going on."

I told him all about Terry, and how he stood me up, and how he tore me down like never before, and I tried to convey to my friend just how hopeless and desperate I felt. But even as I was saying those things, I knew I was making the argument *against* ending my life.

"No, you don't need that," my friend said. "You're just going through emotions, Antoinette. Let me come down and we'll talk it over."

My friend came down and we sat in my car and we talked things over, and in this way he was an angel to me that night. God sent someone to stand between me and the worst choice I could have made. God does that, you know. He puts people in our path for a reason.

Nothing my friend could say, however, made me feel much better. I was still hurt and confused and angry. I left my friend's house and drove to see Terry's aunt, and I spoke with her for a while, but I knew I couldn't stay there either. I had too much rage in my heart, and I was afraid I might do something crazy. I knew there was only one place in the world where I could be safe from myself.

I got in my car and drove as fast as I could to my church.

"Lord, speed my spirit," I prayed. "My flesh is weak and I've got to get to You now."

GOD PUTS PEOPLE IN OUR PATH FOR A REASON.

When I walked into the church, Apostle Tuff was right in the middle of a New Year's Eve service. I sat in a back pew and cried as quietly as I could. I didn't hear anything Apostle said, or any Scriptures or any songs or anything, because I was crying so hard. I just sat in the back and wept through the whole service.

And yet, just as I'd hoped, being in the church was helping. Being in the presence of God was making a difference. I was calming down. I was getting ahold of myself. Light, not blackness, was coming over me. The mountain of pain was being lifted, ever so slightly. But just that little bit of breathing room was all I needed.

Near the end of the service I looked up from the floor and fixed my eyes on the big white cross behind Apostle Tuff. I had something to say to God.

"God," I said, maybe aloud, maybe not, "if You allow me to live through this day, I promise You that next year will be my heaven, because this year was my hell."

"And God," I went on, "if You allow me to live through this day, I promise I will give everything to You and turn my life over to You and get on with the life You want for me."

"And God," I said, "if You allow me to live through this day, I will release Terry and I will let him go. You, God, will be my husband now."

Not too long after that, the service ended. I stayed in the church for a while and spoke with Apostle and hugged a few fellow worshipers and wished them a happy new year. I drove home and went upstairs and got in bed, and just before I turned out the lights I looked at the clock and it said 1:22 a.m.

The day was over. It was 2013. I was still alive. God had saved me again.

Only recently did it occur to me that the night Michael Hill snapped and threatened to kill his brother—New Year's Eve 2012—was the very same night I snapped and wanted to kill myself.

//////

God heard me in the church that night, and in the months after He saved my life I vowed to make it worth His while. Being on my

BEING IN THE
PRESENCE OF GOD WAS
MAKING A DIFFERENCE.
I WAS CALMING DOWN.
I WAS GETTING AHOLD
OF MYSELF. LIGHT,
NOT BLACKNESS, WAS
COMING OVER ME.

own was all new territory for me, and I was scared to death, but even so I had no choice—a deal is a deal. I would have to find a way to base my life around me and not around Terry. For the first time in my life, I would have to live for myself.

I decided to go ahead and start the transportation business Terry and I talked about starting together. The first step was going to the motor coach conference we'd planned to go to before the money went to fix Terry's feet. But, once again, I didn't have enough money to register for the conference or rent a hotel room. A couple of years earlier, when things began to fall apart between Terry and me, and when the medical bills for him and Derrick really put us in a crunch, we were forced to file for bankruptcy—not the kind that wipes out your debt but the kind where you still have to pay what you owe, only now you have a repayment plan. After that, every month was a struggle to make ends meet. And after Terry moved out and started spending money on his own new life, my finances got even tighter. The motor coach conference was going to cost me five hundred dollars, and I just didn't have it.

That is when God sent me another angel who gave me the money.

"Marie, this is my personal investment in you," this angel told me. "I want to bless you with this."

God, it seemed, was keeping His end of the bargain.

I went to the conference and I started my own small business, trying to get it off the ground while still working three other jobs— as a bookkeeper at McNair, as an after-school substitute, and as a sponsor with the Cool Girls group. I worked pretty much from sunup to sundown, and beyond, and when I felt weak and fearful I would open my Bible and let God give me the words I needed to hear. "Trust in the Lord with all thine heart; and lean not unto thine own understanding," Proverbs 3:5–6 says. "In all thy ways acknowledge him, and he shall direct thy paths."

But what about the money, Lord? What do I do when I can't pay my bills? When Derrick's medical bills and my utility bills and my mortgage bill and my own medical bills all come through the front door at the same time, and I don't have but a few dollars in my checking account?

It is right there in Philippians 4:11–13, the Lord answered. "Not that I speak in respect of want: for I have learned, in whatsoever state I am, therewith to be content. I know both how to be abased, and I know how to abound: every where and in all things I am instructed both to be full and to be hungry, both to abound and to suffer need. I can do all things through Christ which strengtheneth me."

Be happy with what you have, God tells us, and rejoice in Him always, and have faith you can endure the trials that will only make you stronger.

But at the same time, it says in Philippians 4:6–7, speak to God and let Him know what you need. "Be careful for nothing; but in every thing by prayer and supplication with thanksgiving let your requests be made known unto God. And the peace of God, which passeth all understanding, shall keep your hearts and minds through Christ."

And when I believed the only thing I needed was something I couldn't have—Terry—God sent me another Scripture, Philippians

4:19: "But my God shall supply all your need according to his riches in glory by Christ Jesus."

I did not need Terry. All I needed was God.

That is how I went about my first few months alone, by rejoicing in God for what I had and praying to Him for what I needed. I took a free business class through my church and another one at a local business academy, and slowly I learned the ins and outs of starting a business. And when I got a paycheck, no matter how small it was, I went to the church and I offered my tithe, because that is what God instructs us to do—not to give millions but to *give what we can, as much as we can.* "Honour the Lord with thy substance," reads Proverbs 3:9–10, "and with the firstfruits of all thine increase. So shall thy barns be filled with plenty, and presses shall burst out with new wine."

FOR THE FIRST TIME IN MY LIFE, I WOULD HAVE TO LIVE FOR MYSELF.

Those first few months after God saved my life were some of the hardest months I ever had, and there were many, many times I still thought of Terry and wished he would come home.

But looking back now, I can see that during those months I was also getting stronger. I was developing a bit of a shell. I wasn't letting Terry's endless back-and-forth be a part of my life, and I wasn't giving him more chances to tear me down to the ground. He would call me, and I would answer, and sometimes we'd speak just like before, going over the same old territory, hashing out who was to blame. And, sometimes, he would even tell me he still loved me. But having him flitter in and out of my life just wasn't good for me. One day, during one of our typical phone conversations, the time came when I'd had enough.

"You know what, Terry?" I said. "I am no longer going to give you control of my life. I am taking it back. I am going to finish what God started for both of us. You decided to jump off the boat, and I cannot make you stay on that boat, but I can decide to stay on it, and that's what I'm going to do. So don't you call me anymore with none of this nonsense."

"Fine," Terry said. "It's over with us. You go about your business."

A couple of days later the phone rang again, and I saw it was Terry calling. I let the phone ring until it stopped ringing. Then I put the phone away.

It was the first time I'd ever not answered a phone call from Terry.

The battle between Terry and me turned from me wanting him to come back to me to wanting him to sign the divorce papers. But Terry proved just as stubborn when it came to ending our marriage as he was when it came to making it work.

The few times we talked I begged him to come over and sign the divorce papers I'd had drawn up, but he always found a reason not to come. I couldn't understand why, if he didn't love me anymore, he wouldn't just let me be. But the truth is there were a lot of things swirling around in Terry's head I never could understand.

After a lot of fights on the phone, I finally got Terry to agree to meet me in a parking lot to sign the divorce papers. At the time he was living in the house he'd told me he moved into by himself, but which was really for him and the other woman and her daughter—Terry's new family. He would stop by to see Derrick now and then, but I knew my son was feeling almost as abandoned as I was. The day I was supposed to meet Terry in the parking lot I took Derrick with me, so he could see his daddy.

Terry never showed. I called him on the phone and we got into one of our screaming matches. I almost forgot Derrick was in the car with me, until all of a sudden my son looked over at me and said, "Momma!" very loudly.

I stopped talking and looked at him.

"Momma," he said, "I love you and I don't mean to disrespect you, but hang up that phone."

I looked at the cell phone in my hand, but for some reason I could not disconnect the call.

"Just hang it up," Derrick said. "I know you love him, Momma. And I know how hard this is. But you have to let him go. You have to let him go."

I stared at the phone in my hand. Derrick kept talking.

"Momma, you are happier now without him than I ever seen you in twenty years. It's time for you to live for yourself and let God guide you. Momma, you can take my social security check and pay for the divorce yourself. You just gotta let him go. We had a good day today, and we're not going to let Daddy's foolishness ruin it."

Here was my son, the one who'd gone through trial after trial and never lost his joyous spirit, trying to help me get through my own trial. Here was the boy who couldn't see and couldn't walk and faced a life no child should face, speaking words of grace and wisdom and charity and love. I sat with the phone in my hand and I could only think of one thing to say to him.

"But he's your father," I said.

Derrick took one of my hands in his.

"Momma, you gotta realize something. I've been a disappointment to Daddy since the day I was born. He wanted a son who was whole, and he got me. I couldn't do what he wanted me to do—I couldn't fulfill the destiny he wanted for his own life. And once he realized that, he only tolerated me, Momma. He didn't love me, he just accepted me. He's not my daddy anymore."

I hung up on Terry. Then I hugged my son. I was crying and so was he.

"Let's face it, Momma," he said to me. "If it wasn't for you, I wouldn't have nobody."

I called in a sheriff to serve Terry with the divorce papers. I arranged for Terry to drop off a suitcase my son could take to college with him, and I told the sheriff to be on the lookout for a big blue Navigator. I watched from my bedroom window as Terry pulled up and got out of the car, and the sheriff came over and handed him the papers. Whether Terry liked it or not, the divorce process had now been activated.

A few weeks later, while we were still married, Terry moved to South Carolina. He never told me he was moving; I found out from one of his co-workers. Our no longer being in the same state made the divorce process more complicated, but I made sure it never bogged down too much. Eventually, we set a date for Terry to come back to Georgia so we could sit with a mediator and hammer out the details of our divorce.

I was already in the office of my lawyer when Terry walked in. I hadn't seen him in a while, and he looked heavier and more haggard than I remembered. He looked tired and stressed, and I remember feeling sorry for him. We got down to business, and the mediation went quickly. I got to keep the house, and all Terry wanted was his toolbox, his basketball trophies from high school, and a framed photo of his mother. Terry walked out of the meeting without saying good-bye and took a bus back to South Carolina. I went home and got in bed. The divorce was all but official now. All we needed was for the final paperwork to come through.

I got back to my lonely life at home. By then LaVita was away at law school, and I had enrolled Derrick in a college in Louisiana. It hadn't been easy to let Derrick go to a mainstream college so far away from home, and I worried all the time how he would manage there by himself. But there were special programs in place to help him, and for the most part Derrick was just like any other student. He went to his classes, hung out with his roommates, went to dinner with his friends. I had taught Derrick to fend for himself, and that's just what he did—he got by.

Not long after the mediation meeting with Terry, my son called me from his dorm room in Louisiana. It was Father's Day 2013, and I could tell as soon as I heard Derrick's voice that something was wrong.

"Momma, I'm not doing good," he said. "Momma, I'm having problems breathing."

I had emergency numbers in Louisiana written down on a pad by the phone and I told him to call for help while I held on. I stayed on the phone with my son while paramedics put him in an ambulance and rushed him to the hospital. When he had to hang up I waited for a few minutes, then called the nurse's station at the hospital. They went and checked on my son.

After a long wait one of the nurses called me back.

"He's in a room here," she told me, "and he's doing fair."

I asked the nurse if I needed to come down right away, and she said no, to let them work on him for a while. Whatever was wrong didn't seem too serious at that time. I called the nurse's station all night long to see how Derrick was doing. The next morning, when I called for the tenth time, one of the nurses told me, "He's calling for you, Mrs. Tuff. He's crying and calling out for his momma."

I hung up and got ready to go to my son.

I had never driven any long distance without Terry in the car with me, and I didn't think I could make it all the way to Louisiana—over five hundred miles—by myself. I checked my bank account and saw I didn't even have enough for the Greyhound bus ticket. I called a friend and begged her to lend me the money, and, bless her, she did. I went to the bus depot and got on the bus and took the fifteen-hour overnight ride to Louisiana. I got to the hospital the Tuesday after Father's Day.

When I walked into Derrick's hospital room I was shocked. He was hooked up to tubes and he was wearing an adult diaper. He

168

was on medicine to regulate his heart, which was beating wildly, and he was on more medicine to prevent convulsions. He was sweating profusely because he had a high fever—so high the nurses wheeled in a giant fan and trained it on him to try and cool him down. Even so he was so hot his skin was starting to peel away from his body. His breathing was labored and he wasn't urinating, and one by one his organs were shutting down.

"What are you trying to tell me??" I screamed at one of the doctors.

But I already knew what he was telling me. He was telling me my son was dying.

If the doctors couldn't get his fever down—and figure out what was wrong with him—Derrick was going to die. I asked for a cot and slept beside my son that night, and the next night, and the night after that, praying as hard as I'd ever prayed in my life. But nothing was working. My son's organs kept failing him. In another day or two, I would surely lose him.

On my third day at the hospital, my cell phone rang. It was my lawyer calling.

"Good news," she said. "The papers came in. Your divorce is final."

//

But the Lord is faithful;
he will strengthen you and
guard you from evil.

2 Thessalonians 3:3 RSV

//

CHAPTER NINE

TUESDAY, AUGUST 20, 2013

The gunman spoke so softly I couldn't hear what he was saying. "Your name is Michael what?" I said. "Michael Hill?"

"Yeah," he said. "I was here before. I was with the kids from the high school that were playing the drums."

I still couldn't hear him clearly. I thought he said someone from the high school came in and planted a gun.

"The kids from the high school playing drums," he repeated.

I finally understood. Once in a while a high school band came in and played with our elementary school band, and apparently Michael Hill had played the drums in one of those bands. I remembered when the band came, but I could not remember Michael. But I wanted him to know I remembered the music he played.

"So you came with the kids that played the drums?" I said. "You were actually in there doing all of that with them? How awesome. That means I've seen you before then. Okay."

Then I added, "You all play them drums and stuff real good."

"Thank you," Michael said. Then he lay back down on the

floor, facedown, and put his hands behind his back. He was as calm as I'd seen him yet.

"You can tell them to come in now," he said. "I need to go to the hospital."

///////

Hospitals aren't the only places where healing happens. Healing can happen anywhere you find a quiet spot to pray. In my experience prayer is a powerful tool God gave us, and I've seen prayers answered time and time again. At my church we are not skimpy with our prayers. We pray for a lot of different people and things. Every week we actually draw up a list of people to pray for, and then we get together and go right down the list. We pray for the president, we pray for soldiers, for police officers and governors, for commissioners and educators, for people with money problems, people with cancer. Sometimes we pray globally, like for the people in Japan after the tsunami hit. We believe prayers can carry over oceans and halfway around the world.

One time, at my church in Atlanta, we got together to pray for women who wanted children badly but couldn't have them—women who'd been to fertility doctors and tried everything but still couldn't get pregnant. Apostle Tuff called them to the altar and prayed over them, while his wife, Pastor Deborah Tuff, laid her hands on their bellies. "Lord, open up these wombs that have been closed," we prayed.

Nine months later we got a wave of babies, eight or nine in all. After that more women came forward and asked to be prayed over, and nine months after that we got our second wave. Now, when any woman in our church wants to get pregnant, she goes straight to Pastor Deborah and has her lay hands. That woman has a healing touch when it comes to babies.

I had my own first experience with healing prayer right after Derrick was born. The Baptist church of my youth didn't do healings, but people of the Pentecostal faith sure do. Among his many problems, Derrick had a really bad case of asthma, and he was always on ventilators and other breathing treatments. His first couple of years he was in and out of the hospital all the time. I told the nurses, "You ought to give me my own bed, 'cause we're here so much." But the truth is, I could hardly bear to see Derrick struggle and gasp for breath.

When he was three I decided to take Derrick to see Apostle Tuff. Apostle prayed over him for a while, then took a cloth handkerchief and doused it with anointing oil. He prayed over the handkerchief and handed it to me.

"This is his prayer cloth," he said. "You take it home and put it under his pillow every night, and he will stop having asthma attacks."

I had never heard of a prayer cloth. Apostle Tuff directed me to a Scripture that explained what it was. "So that from his body were brought unto the sick handkerchiefs or aprons," it says in Acts 19:12, "and the diseases departed from them, and the evil spirits went out of them."

I took the cloth home and put it under Derrick's pillow, and every night I prayed that cloth would work.

Derrick never had another asthma attack again.

Now, I'm sure some people will say his healing had nothing to do with a piece of cloth. Maybe they'll even say it had nothing to do with prayer. I am not here to try and convince anyone to believe anything. I can only tell you what I saw with my own eyes. Nothing the doctors did could stop my son from having painful asthma attacks. But the prayer cloth did. Coincidence? I don't believe in coincidences, at least not when God is involved. Look, I'm not saying prayers will cure every disease all the time. But I *am* saying prayers can't do a lick of harm, and with my own eyes I have seen them work.

/////

June 2013

At the hospital Derrick was slipping in and out of consciousness. He was hooked up to an IV and a heart monitor and a couple of other machines. He wasn't eating or drinking, and his fever was still dangerously high. His body temperature was so high his skin was peeling off, and he had a rash all over his body. Every once in a while he would have a violent muscle spasm, and a therapist would have to rush in and try and get his body under control.

The doctors ran lots of tests but no one could figure out what was wrong. With each new test that didn't explain anything I got angrier and angrier. I was frustrated the doctors didn't seem as urgent as I was. I'm afraid I became a terror on that hospital floor. I kept calling the nurses and doctors and demanding they run more tests or bring in a specialist. I even looked up the name of the man who owned the hospital and called him directly.

"I'm going to go straight to the news if you don't do something about my son," I said. "Give me someone who knows what he's doing."

Still, no one could figure out what was wrong.

On the second day, I called Derrick's father, because I felt he ought to know his son was dying. I told Terry he should come to the hospital as soon as he could, and Terry mumbled something about doing it, but in the end he never came. The truth is, I wasn't all that surprised.

> I DON'T BELIEVE IN COINCIDENCES, AT LEAST NOT WHEN GOD IS INVOLVED.

"Don't you care about your son?" I asked Terry many times over the years as he was pulling away from his family to start a new one someplace else. "Aren't you worried what'll happen to him?"

"I know you'll take care of him," is all he would say.

But could I?

I became desperate. I was hurt and angry and scared and desperate. What had my son done to deserve this? Why was everything I loved being taken away from me? Derrick and I always had a special bond, just like LaVita and her father. In the early part of Derrick's life I watched over every single detail of his being. I made sure he never felt like a throwaway child, just because he was different from other children. I made sure he had everything anyone else had, and more. If there was only one pork chop left, I made sure Derrick got it and no one else, because I wanted him to eat it and be strong. Sometimes Terry would get jealous of his son. He'd ask me things like, "Why do you put him before me?" or "Why does he get more food than me?"

"It's not like that," I'd explain. "He needs me to look out for him."

And when Terry began pulling away, I spent even more time with Derrick, to make up for what he was losing. I took him to the movies, or to the food court at the mall, or maybe we'd just hang out at the house and talk. There was always an easy, two-way channel open between us. Sometimes he was the sound of my life, like when he sang to me through the bathroom door. Sometimes I was the sound of his—like when his hearing got bad and he couldn't distinguish syllables and words ran together into a jumble of noise, and I became his translator, leaning in and whispering what someone said so he could answer. We were connected in ways no one else could see or understand. I was his strength, and he was mine.

It got to where Derrick's disabilities became invisible to me. The muscles in his legs had atrophied, and at home he would use his arms to swing his body from room to room, up and down stairs, his legs useless and curled up beneath him. With good legs he would have been six feet tall, maybe taller, but now the tallest he ever got was four feet off the ground. His fingers were badly curled, and it was all he could do to hold a fork so he could take in food. When people in the street saw him I am sure they saw a disabled boy.

Derrick performing at the Center for the Visually Impaired.

Derrick at his graduation in 2009 from the Georgia Academy for the Blind. The ceremony was held at the Georgia Music Hall of Fame.

Dekalb County Police SWAT officers and other
first responders running toward Ronald E. McNair
Discovery Learning Academy.

The school was soon surrounded by authorities.

There were hundreds of happy reunions after the siege. Students had been taken by school buses to a nearby Wal-Mart, where parents and other relatives were waiting.

The day after the incident, staff at our local high school expressed their
support. The whole community rallied around McNair Academy.

AC360° Exclusive

CNN's Anderson Cooper surprised me during an interview with a first-time meeting with Kendra McCray, the 9-1-1 dispatcher who was on the phone with me for much of the standoff at McNair. Her composure during the call helped immensely.

A week after the incident, I was humbled to be recognized at a church service by Apostle Ulysses Tuff and his wife, Pastor Deborah.

I'm grateful for all the opportunities to share how God helped me at McNair Academy that day. This photo is from Treasure You, a women's retreat hosted by Pat Smith.

Three months after the incident, I was privileged to speak
at the 2013 CNN Heroes All-Star Tribute.

But I didn't see any of those things. To me he wasn't broken in any way. To me he was just my beautiful Derrick. And maybe, some nights, when he drifted off to sleep, Derrick would dream of running along a beach, or diving into a lake, or kicking a soccer ball. Maybe my son dreamt of being whole. But I never dreamt these things, because I didn't have to. To me, in the harsh, blinding light of reality, my Derrick was already whole.

But now—this. This dreary room, this lonely bed, this sweaty, crumpled pillow beneath his head. My son's twisted, wasting body at the mercy of tubes and pumps. His whole life reduced to this bleak, unfriendly space. He looked so helpless laying there, so small and vulnerable. So *broken*. Everything I'd taught him about fending for himself, about being strong and independent, all of it was meaningless, because here was something he couldn't control. And there I was, by his side but powerless to fix what was wrong. When Terry left me I felt powerless, and that was one of the worst feelings I ever felt. But it was nothing next to what I felt now. This was a deep, wrenching feeling of anguish, of smallness, of an almost childlike rage and injustice. Of wanting to smash the walls with my fists and roll around on the floor. Of wanting to scream and wail and plead, "Why can't I listen to my son sing a gospel song? Why can't I cook him another pork chop? Why can't I have these things? Why? Why?"

"It's not fair," I wanted to cry. "It's just not fair."

But if you are a mother who has been in a situation like this, you know that is not what a mother does. A mother pushes these feelings away—she puts her weight aside—and she gets on with the business at hand. And the business at hand was the business of saving my son. I had no time to get upset about Terry not coming. I didn't have the luxury of feeling sorry for myself for too long. I was in a desperate race against the clock. Every minute Derrick's fever stayed high was another minute closer to him dying. By the third day the stench of death hung heavy in his hospital room. The people who walked in could feel it, too, and I knew many of them couldn't wait to walk out. I had to find a way to chase away that stench. I had to bring life to a place of lingering death.

I searched my brain for any clue, any memory that might help. I remembered that when Derrick was young he was allergic to ibuprofen, so I came up with a homemade remedy whenever he ran a fever. But for the life of me I couldn't remember what the ingredients were. But I had to do something, so I decided to wing it and asked a nurse to bring me some alcohol and vinegar. I mixed them up and I took a piece of cloth and soaked it in the mixture. Then I rubbed the cloth on my son's body anywhere he had a pulse. I rubbed it on his heart and his temple and his neck and his wrists. I kept rubbing him down hour after hour and praying while I did it. Some of the nurses prayed with me, but others gave me looks like I was wasting my time. I didn't care.

"Lord," I prayed, "I'm overwhelmed. I'm scared. Please help me stay strong for my son. Please bring my boy back to me."

I even called Apostle Tuff and held the phone to Derrick's ear so Apostle could pray over him from five hundred miles away. I knew prayers could cross oceans. I expected they could cross a few states.

And I kept touching Derrick with the cloth, his heart, temple, neck, wrists, hour after hour, day and night. I'd sleep for a bit then get back to it. I prayed long and loud and hard, and I worked the cloth until I couldn't feel my hands. "Is anyone among you sick?" it says in James 5:14. "Let him call for the elders of the church, and let them pray over him, anointing him with oil in the name of the Lord" (NKJV). Curing someone with oil might be impossible in the medical world, but even then I knew my son's cure would not come from doctors. "With men it is impossible," Jesus said in Mark 10:27, "but not with God: for with God all things are possible."

I prayed and washed Derrick with that cloth for three days. Still, his body was burning up and his organs were shutting down. His breathing was thin and raspy, and his pulse was weakening. His skin was literally coming off his body, as if he was preparing to leave it. The medical staff looked at me with pity in their eyes. I just kept doing the only thing I knew to do—pray and rub, pray and rub.

And then, on the fifth day Derrick was in the hospital, his fever broke.

////

The nurses were amazed. There was no medical reason why his fever went down. All of a sudden, it just did. Derrick became a little bit more alert, though he still couldn't eat or drink a thing—and we still didn't know what was wrong with him. But as soon as I saw a glimmer of life in his broken body, I knew what I had to do.

I had to get Derrick out of that hospital.

"Lord," I prayed, "I'm overwhelmed. I'm scared. Please help me stay strong for my son. Please bring my boy back to me."

The only way he'd be strong enough to leave was if he started eating something, and that became my mission. Ice chips at first, then tiny spoonfuls of Jell-O. Derrick couldn't keep them down, but I kept forcing him to try.

"Listen to me, baby," I pleaded. "You gotta start eating. That's the only way we're going to get you out of this place. *You gotta start eating.*"

Derrick, still too weak to talk much, let me spoon bits of Jell-O into his mouth. After a while, he kept some of them down.

When his fever dropped a little more, I got an idea. I called some of his friends in Louisiana and told them to come to the hospital and bring foods Derrick liked to eat. They showed up with pizza and chicken dinners and hamburgers. Derrick took small bites, and he kept them down. And every time the tiniest piece of pizza or chicken disappeared, my heart sang a heavenly song of joy. With each bite my spirits soared higher. In hospitals victories are sometimes measured in tiny sips and bites. But they are the sweetest victories of all.

I decided that as soon as Derrick was strong enough, I would check him out of the hospital and get him home, even if doctors hadn't figured out what was wrong with him. I didn't need their approval and I didn't care if I got it. All I needed was for Derrick to get out of bed and get in a wheelchair. But even after he started eating he was still too weak to pull that off. So with the help of the nurses I would lift Derrick out of bed and get him into his chair. His body was heavy, and my back nearly gave out every time I tried to lift him, but still we kept pushing and pushing to get him in his chair. It was like I was trying to *will* the life back into my son's body.

181

Finally, after many tries, we managed to get Derrick into the wheelchair. But he couldn't sit up for too long, and he had to work hard not to slide out and crumple to the ground. I realized right then I wouldn't be able to take Derrick back home on a bus. There was no way he could endure a fifteen-hour trip in a cramped bus seat. The only way he could travel would be in a car, where he'd have room to lie down. But, like I said, I had never driven any distance greater than ten or twenty miles without my husband in the car with me. I had no confidence I could handle busy highways packed with speeding trucks, and especially not at night. But what choice did I have? Terrified or not, the only way to get Derrick home was for me to drive him. So I rented a car, and I started praying for God to drive with me.

Just a few hours before we were set to check out, a doctor came into the room.

"Your son has a blood infection," he said.

They had finally figured out what was wrong—a serious blood infection. They started Derrick on two different antibiotics and gave me a prescription for a third to take home with me. The bill for the pills alone was eight hundred dollars, which I didn't have. But I wasn't worried about money. All I cared about was getting Derrick home.

I went to the rental place and drove back to the hospital in a midsize car. Slowly and carefully I got Derrick into his wheelchair and out of the hospital, and then I sort of pushed him into the front passenger seat of the rental. He was so much better than he'd been just two days earlier, but he was still very weak, and still in a lot of pain. I prayed that God might give us safe passage, and I pulled out on the road. Before too long Derrick felt uncomfortable, so I pulled over and got him into the back of the car. He lay across both seats with pillows everywhere, propping him up.

"This is good, Momma," he told me. "This is better."

I prayed to God again and got on US-65, heading for Interstate-20.

I wish I hadn't been such a chicken about driving, but I was. Like so many other things in my life, driving was something I always did with Terry. If he was in the car with me I could handle a highway. But without him I was lost. I did my best to not let Derrick see how terrified I was, but I guess all the praying I was doing tipped him off.

"You all right, Momma?" he asked.

I was the one who should have been asking him that, but he was asking me. He hadn't complained about how much pain he was in, except to say he wanted to get in the back, but I knew he couldn't be feeling very well at all. And yet he was asking me if I was all right.

"Yes, baby," I said. "Everything's okay."

My son saw through the lie. He saw I was scared to death we wouldn't make it home. I feared an accident, or bad weather, or if I fell asleep, or a drunk driver, or just an eighteen-wheeler rushing by too close. There were few times in my life I was as scared as I was in that car. But I had to keep going, keep eating up the miles. My hands squeezed that steering wheel like it was made of gold.

"Momma," Derrick said after a while, "want to try this?"

He handed me a little dock for plugging in an iPad or iPhone.

"That way you can listen to your music while you drive," he said.

I put the dock on the seat next to me and plugged my iPad in. I pressed play and a beautiful gospel song came on. I sang along with the song, and when he felt strong enough Derrick sang along, too. I sang along to every gospel song for the next ten hours, pausing only to pray and ask God to guide us home, and once to go to the bathroom and get Derrick some water to drink.

And in this way, praying and singing and squeezing the wheel, I got my child home.

/////

Derrick spent the rest of June and then July of 2013 at home with me, recovering. The antibiotics did their job, and each day he got stronger. His old joyful, playful self was back before I knew it.

"Come on over here, Momma, I wanna sing you a song," he'd say. Or he'd tell me to climb on his wheelchair and he'd wheel me around the kitchen. Despite all my other problems I felt truly happy—maybe happier than I had in years—every time Derrick hugged me or held my hand or sang me a song. And I tried to forget just how close I came to losing him. But even though I felt joy in my heart, don't think I stopped praying once my son was better. I prayed just as hard to give thanks. And I prayed for all the other people who had their own Derricks, that God might smile on them like He smiled on us.

That summer I did everything I could to get my life back on track. Terry was gone now, living in another state and not my husband anymore. Every time I thought about that it struck me as impossible—how could Terry *not* be my husband? But he wasn't, simple as that. What we had for thirty-three years was over and done. Sometimes it didn't seem real, and some nights I missed him terribly. Sometimes I'd wake up in the middle of the night shocked to discover I was alone. But none of that changed the facts. Like it or not, I was on my own.

I jumped back into getting my little transportation company going, but it wasn't easy, mainly because I didn't have much money to work with. Terry was paying the monthly bankruptcy bill, but that was all the help I was getting. And Derrick's medical bills were piling up. I kept working my three jobs and paying a bill here and there and pushing my business a little closer to launching. Every day was a crazy juggling act. Most of the time I felt totally lost and uncertain and afraid.

It was in the middle of all this chaos that Apostle Tuff started his sermon series about anchoring yourself in God. Hebrews 6:18–19 urges those "who have fled for refuge to lay hold upon the hope set before us: Which hope we have as an anchor of the soul, both sure and steadfast." Whatever our torment, whatever our struggle, we will not lose our footing in Christ because He has given us an anchor—He has given us hope. And as long as we keep laboring in faith, God will not let us be lost. *God will not let go of us.* "Be ye steadfast, unmovable, always abounding in the work of the Lord," 1 Corinthians 15:58 tells us, "forasmuch as ye know that your labor is not in vain." *Steadfast and unmovable*, I would tell myself. *My soul is anchored in Christ.*

That August my workdays lasted as long as the sun, and beyond. Getting up at 5:00 a.m., some quiet time with my prayers and my music, talking to God and listening for an answer, whipping up a hearty breakfast for Derrick, wrapping up his lunch and dinner, showering and picking an outfit, showing up at McNair Academy at the stroke of 7:00 a.m. Working all day, working some more after school, mentoring the Cool Girls after that. Getting home just before dusk, paying some bills, working on my business, hugging my son. Some more quiet time, a few more prayers, some gospel music lulling me to sleep. Getting up before the sun and doing it all over again.

STEADFAST AND UNMOVABLE, I WOULD TELL MYSELF. MY SOUL IS ANCHORED IN CHRIST.

On the morning of August 20, 2013, I picked the simplest outfit I could: a brown halter-top dress, no sleeves, brown high heels, a necklace, and a bracelet. My glasses, which I need for up-close reading. No jacket, since the day was hot. And into my 2003 red GMC Envoy, out of my garage and onto Interstate-20. Pull into McNair Academy and park in my space, which has a little sign that says, "Bookkeeper." Walk a few feet and arrive at work at 7:00 on the nose.

Settle into my office, which has changed in recent months. It used to be full of photos of Terry and me and the kids. Probably twenty framed photos, all of them showing a happy couple or happy kids or a happy family. But most of those photos are gone now, or at least all the ones that had Terry in them. Now there are only photos of me and my children, or my children by themselves. Photos of the kids at different school events. Photos of the three of us on Halloween. I don't remember what I did with the photos of Terry. They might be in a box in my garage. They might not be.

I grabbed my mail on the way to my office and put the handful of letters on my desk. Bills, mostly, from vendors and suppliers, Office Depot, an insurance company, things like that. It was early in the new semester, so most of my morning was going to go to entering the students' applications into the school database. Each year we get a big new crop of kindergarten kids, and they come with a lot of paperwork. I helped a teacher with some matter, and I paid some bills, and I logged a few applications into the computer, and after a while I took a break and got a cup of coffee and a bowl of Cheerios from the cafeteria.

Not long after that the principal stopped by my office and asked if I could fill in for the receptionist at 12:30. It's a rotating thing, and all of us—paraprofessionals, administrators, staffers—fill in when we can. I had no lunch plans that day, so I said sure. He could have asked a number of other people to fill in, but for whatever reason he asked me.

I spent the rest of the morning taking care of paperwork. At 12:15, I started to get ready to go up to the front desk. I thought about going to the bathroom but I decided I didn't need to go that badly. And anyway, I could go later.

Everything was in order. Nothing seemed out of place. The day was unfolding like any other.

And then, at 12:20 p.m., I got the phone call that made the mountains shake.

/////

It came in on my cell. I didn't recognize the number. I said hello and a woman answered and told me she was from my bank. There was some kind of problem.

"What's wrong?" I asked, my heart pushing its way into my throat. The bank officer told me what was happening in a flat, mechanical tone.

She told me I was losing everything.

There was an issue with our bankruptcy repayment plan. It seemed the bank was canceling it because of a lack of payment, and a balance of $14,000 was due immediately. If I couldn't come up with the $14,000—which, Lord knows, I couldn't—then my house and my car and my furniture would all be repossessed. *My house and my car and my furniture.* Everything I had.

As soon as I heard that I went into some kind of shock. The rest of the conversation was a blur. I wasn't even clear on why this was happening, or what had gone wrong, but that didn't matter—all that mattered was that Derrick and I were being kicked out of our house. How could this be happening to me? Hadn't I had to endure enough?

Fourteen thousand dollars? I had no hope of ever getting my hands on that kind of money. I told that to the bank officer and she told me I had exactly ten days. After that there was nothing she could do.

The tears ran down my face even before I knew I was crying. I'd been kicked in the gut a whole bunch of times by then, but this kick hurt bad as any. With no car I couldn't go to work and earn money. With no house I couldn't put a roof over Derrick's head. Is that where we were going to end up—out on the street? Panic and terror seized my whole body, and when I got up to close my office door I nearly fell because my legs were so weak. Yes, the Bible tells us to "be steadfast and unmovable," but how could I be those things now? I felt anything *but* steadfast and unmovable—I felt weak and adrift. I understood hope was my anchor, but at that moment I felt completely hopeless. I hung up the call and put my head in my hands.

"What in the world are we going to do now, Lord?" I said aloud. "What in the world are we going to do now?"

At 12:35 my office phone rang. It was the receptionist, wondering where I was. I pulled myself together as quickly as I could. I dried my eyes and took a quick peek at a small mirror I kept in my desk to see how red they were. I took three or four deep breaths and asked God to give me strength to get through the next few hours. Then, as if nothing had happened—as if my life hadn't been turned upside down yet again—I walked out of my office and went to the front to sit in for the receptionist.

And just a few minutes after I got there the front door opened and a man walked in. I looked up and saw the rifle.

Michael Hill was back on the floor, facedown, hands behind his back. His rifle and bullets and book bag were neatly lined up on the counter a few feet away. At that moment he seemed more resigned and tired than angry. I knew the time to end this was upon us.

"You can tell them to come in now," Michael said. "I need to go to the hospital."

I got back on the phone with the 9-1-1 dispatcher.

"He says they can come on in now," I told her. "He needs to go to the hospital."

"Okay," the dispatcher said.

"He doesn't have any weapons on him or anything like that," I went on. "He's laying on the floor, and he doesn't have any weapons and he's got everything out of his pocket. The only thing he has on is his belt. Everything is out of his pockets and sitting on the counter so all we need to do is, they can come and I'll buzz them in so he'll know they're here."

> HE SEEMED MORE RESIGNED AND TIRED THAN ANGRY. I KNEW THE TIME TO END THIS WAS UPON US.

"Okay," the dispatcher said, "one moment."

"She said she's going to let them know," I told Michael. "She's going to let them know to come on in and take you to the hospital, okay?"

Suddenly Michael pushed himself up into a sitting position again.

"Do they want me to go out there with my hands up?" he asked.

"No, you stay right there," I said. "You're fine. Stay right where you are."

But Michael was up on his feet now. Suddenly he was agitated again. The rifle and the bullets were within reach. He turned and walked toward the counter. I didn't know what he was going to do.

"Is it okay if I get some water?" Michael asked.

"He wants to know if he can get some of his water," I said to the dispatcher. I wanted Michael to know the lines of communication were open, and that we were getting close to letting the police in.

"Yes, go ahead," I told him.

Michael went to his book bag and took out the bottle and took another long drink. The office was still strangely quiet. We had no way of knowing where the officers were or when they would come in, and the not knowing was starting to anger Michael. I tried to take his mind off all the waiting.

"Michael Hill?" I said. "That's your name?"

"Yeah," he said.

"Guess what, Michael," I said. "My last name is Hill. My mom was a Hill." This was true, my mother's maiden name was Hill. I was about to tell him we might be related somewhere down the line, but before I could, Michael started pacing in the middle of the room again.

"What are they waiting for?" he said loudly. "What's taking so long?"

I got back on with the dispatcher, who told me the police were on their way.

"She said she is getting them now," I told Michael. "They're coming, they're coming. Go ahead and lay down."

Then Michael reached into his book bag once more.

"Don't . . ." I said.

He pulled something out of the bag.

It was his cell phone.

"Okay, you just got your phone," I said. "Okay, that's fine." I went back to talking to the dispatcher. "Tell them to come on," I said. "Come on in. He just got his cell phone, that's all he got, is his phone. It's just him, okay? It's just him."

Slowly, Michael lowered himself to the floor. He lay his head on the carpet like it was a pillow, and he put his hands behind his back. I didn't know how long he would stay down this time. He hadn't been able to shut off his anger and emotions for any real length of time. We only had small intervals when he was relatively calm. I prayed the police would come in during one of those times.

Out of the corner of my eye I saw some movement through the small, narrow window in the door that led to the hallway and the back of the school. I made sure Michael couldn't see me before I turned my head and looked.

Through the window I saw someone dressed completely in black, including a black helmet. He had a big rifle in his hand, commando-style, and he was crouching and inching his way closer and closer toward the door. Then I saw another man in black behind him, and then several more. There must have been ten or twelve of them and they were moving as a pack, slowly and quietly gaining ground, heading straight toward my office—straight toward Michael and me.

The sight of them took my breath away. Every nerve in my body felt electric. I looked down at Michael, who was starting to stir again. If he got up now and saw what I saw, who knows what he would do? It would only take him a second or two to grab his gun and start shooting.

The men got closer, eerily silent. No sound of shuffling boots or clinking metal. Michael lay on the floor, restless. When the men got within three or four feet of the door I heard them for the first time—a muted, rustling sound of footsteps. I looked down at Michael and I saw he heard it, too. He lifted his head up off the floor a few inches. The men got closer, so close I could see the visors on their helmets.

The door flew open and the swarm began.

///////////////////////////////////////

Faith is the confidence that
what we hope for will actually
happen; it gives us assurance
about things we cannot see.

Hebrews 11:1 NLT

///////////////////////////////////////

CHAPTER TEN

TUESDAY,
AUGUST 20, 2013

The men rushed in one or two at a time, and in an instant there were eight or nine or ten armed officers in the room, maybe more. They came in crouching behind their wide shields, in case they were met with gunfire. They pointed their rifles and yelled commands and darted swiftly from one spot to the next. Three officers dropped themselves right on top of Michael, smothering him, one across his torso, another across his legs, the third atop them all, pinning them down. One of them grabbed Michael's hands, which were already behind his back, and handcuffed them there. They did these things with force and speed and purpose. Michael did not resist or say a word.

I stayed in my chair behind the desk and tried not to move a muscle. I can't say I felt relief when the SWAT team came crashing in. If anything, I felt more fear. I'd never been around so many drawn and loaded weapons in my life, and it was not a comfortable feeling. At least the officers had shields and helmets and riot gear. But in my own way, I was protected, too. "The Lord is my strength and my shield," it says in Psalm 28:7. "My heart trusted in him, and I am helped."

At first the officers paid no attention to me as they went about their business of arresting Michael and securing the room. They opened all the doors leading into the office and ran in and out and confirmed there was no second gunman and no booby traps. One of the men on the ground searched Michael's pockets, while another went through his book bag on the counter. Another yelled at him: "Do you have any other weapons?" Michael said no. Another officer took the AK-47 away.

Then Michael was hoisted to his feet, and the officers patted him down and searched him some more, and then, before I knew it, two men hustled him out of the room through the front door. I never got to say anything final to him. All told, I was in that room with Michael for somewhere around one hour—maybe the most excruciating hour of each of our lives. But now, in a flash, he was gone.

I heard a voice somewhere yell out, "We are clear!"

Almost immediately the room became a crime scene. Different officers focused on different areas, doing whatever they had to do. They marked off shell casings and studied the bullet hole in the carpet. One of the officers, her visor up now, came over to where I was sitting.

"Are you okay?" she asked.

"Yes," I said, "I'm okay."

She looked at me for a second, then said, "You're shaking."

I looked down at my legs. They were doing a crazy dance. My whole body was trembling uncontrollably. I looked back up at the officer.

"I have to go to the bathroom," I explained.

/////

Even with all the commotion, Shirley Caesar popped back in my brain and sang me "Hold My Mule." And I felt like praising God, too, so I sang along with Shirley in my mind. Song or no song, God knows I'd held my mule long enough.

"Everything is clear," the SWAT officer said to me. "You can go to the bathroom."

Slowly I rose to my feet, bracing myself with my hands against the desktop. Immediately I realized that if I let go, I'd crumple to the floor. My legs had no strength at all. They were too weak to move my body. I sat back down, still shaking. *Lord, hold my mule.*

Another officer came over and asked if I was okay. Then he asked some questions about what happened. I answered them as best I could.

"You did a great job," he said when he was finished.

Three or four more officers came over to talk to me. I guess there were four or five different divisions involved in the raid; local police, the sheriff's office, a SWAT team, state troopers. And the person in charge of each division came over to talk to me. All of them made sure I was okay, and all of them told me what a great job I did.

Finally a police officer handed me a pad of paper and asked me to write my statement. I sat there, still shaking, and tried to think what to write. I tried to remember all the things that happened and all the things I said, but I could barely remember any of it. I couldn't recall the conversation I'd just had with Michael. I'm sure people will say that's because I was still in shock, and maybe that's true, but even then it didn't surprise me that I couldn't remember my own words.

Because, you see, they weren't my words. It was God speaking through me.

I grabbed a pen and scribbled something to start my statement. I wrote, "The gunman entered the building. . . ."

//////

What I didn't write was my perception of how I handled the whole situation. Because if I wrote that, I would have written, "The entire time I was screaming at the top of my lungs, I was so scared."

It took me a long while to look back on those two hours and picture myself any way other than hysterical. It took a few hours before I was able to remember just how calm I had been. Later, when I heard the tape of my 9-1-1 call to police, I noticed how there wasn't a trace of fear or panic in my voice. It truly sounded like I was talking to and about a student who had misbehaved or missed a class. I knew it was me talking because I recognized my voice. But the words and the demeanor did not seem to be mine. It had not been my conscious decision to talk and act that way.

I just opened my mouth and those words came out, in the exact order and exact tone that they needed to be.

I can't say I was even aware of talking at all. Like I said, it was God speaking through me.

But that isn't the kind of thing you put in a police statement.

I still hadn't had the chance to properly exhale. My body was still shaking and I was still in a daze. And, of course, I still had to go to the bathroom. In the office, the swarm continued—officers coming in and out, scooping up evidence, taking measurements, what have you. I suddenly felt the urge to get out of that room. I quickly finished my statement—figuring I could add to it later—and tried once again to rise to my weakened feet.

Just then an officer came over and told me we had to leave right away. "The gunman parked his car in front of the school, and we're searching it now," he said. "We want to get everyone away from the front."

Miraculously, my legs went back to working. Two officers helped me out of the office, into the hallway, and to the media center a few feet away. I walked in and saw several people sitting there nervously, including the receptionist whom I'd filled in for and a handful of teachers. When they saw me walk in, they got up and asked me a million questions.

"Oh my, are you okay?"

> IT WAS GOD SPEAKING THROUGH ME. BUT THAT ISN'T THE KIND OF THING YOU PUT IN A POLICE STATEMENT.

"What happened in there?"

"Did he shoot at you?"

"Did you have any chance to run?"

They wanted to know every detail, and I guess I would have, too, if I hadn't lived it myself. But I was in no condition to stand there and recreate the standoff. I wasn't stable on my feet and my mind was still racing and my legs were still shaking because I was still holding my mule.

"I can't talk right now," I said, slumping into an open chair. "I just have to get my nerves back together." I sat in that chair and felt the heaviness of my body. I looked up at the ceiling and tried, for the first time, to exhale—but I couldn't. Everything was still too hectic. We could hear sirens outside and the sound of officers running around, and there was still a real feeling of tension in the air. I had no idea where the children were or what had happened to them. It did not feel like we were on the other side of this nightmare just yet.

After two or three quiet minutes, I got up, walked to the back of the media center, and went into the private restroom.

And it was there, in the restroom, that I looked in the mirror and braced myself against the sink, and for the first time spoke aloud to God. "Thank You for giving me the words. Thank You for guiding me through it. Thank You, God, for sparing my life yet again."

Then I exhaled deeply and finally went to the bathroom.

When I came out I saw one of the officers was back in the media center.

"We have to leave now," he said, with urgency in his voice.

"What's going on?" someone asked.

"One of the dogs got a hit of something in the gunman's car," the officer said. "It could be a bomb. We need to clear everyone *now*."

/////

Several officers hurriedly led the group of us to the back of the school, away from the front entrance. I heard one of them say the gunman's car was parked in a handicapped spot in the row nearest the school, right next to a red truck in a reserved spot. It took me a moment to realize the red truck was my GMC.

Michael had parked next to me.

We were led down one flight of stairs, to the ground floor (the front entrance at McNair actually leads to the second floor), and we left the building through a back door. Behind the school there is a chain link fence that separates the school property from a neighbor's backyard. I saw a big hole had been cut in the fence, and the officers directed us through the hole.

When I first announced the Intruder Alert over the intercom, most of the teachers had their children get under their desks, which is what they're supposed to do. Most of them probably sang and prayed with the children while they waited. But at some point, I later learned, while Michael and I were going through our drama in the front office, several brave teachers began leading their children into the hallway and out the back and through the hole in the fence and into the neighbor's backyard. News footage would later show neat rows of children holding hands and hustling through the fence to safety.

It did not feel like
we were on the
other side of this
nightmare just yet.

Now we made our way through the same hole. I noticed the neighbor, a sweet elderly woman, had set up some chairs and was bringing food and water to anyone who needed it. I found a spot in her yard and stood there for a moment, gathering my thoughts. The warm air and the hot sun felt good on my skin.

Before long a police officer came over and asked me to write another statement. He walked me to his police cruiser nearby, and I got in the back seat and started writing again. My second statement was probably a little more thorough than the first, but I'm sure I missed a lot of stuff. While I was writing the officer asked me some questions. I tried my best to concentrate, but it wasn't easy. My brain was still too cloudy from the shock of it all.

Sometime that afternoon I learned there was no bomb in Michael's car. I also learned no one had been hurt or killed that day. Michael hadn't gone on some earlier rampage, and he hadn't hit anyone when he shot out of the school. All the children were safe and sound and most of them were already back with their parents. The crisis at McNair Academy was over.

The hours after the standoff ended were something of a blur. A lot of different people were prying me for information. I got a call from a local news anchor who wanted to interview me. They told me the news station had rented a hotel room nearby where we could do the interview. It would be a good place for me to get away from all the craziness, she said. That sounded good to me, and I agreed. For the moment, the police were done with me, and I was free to go wherever I wished. I just didn't know where to go.

I did the interview for the local news station, and I'd have to look at the tape to tell you what I said. The only thing I can remember is that I thanked God for speaking through me and guiding us all to safety. After the interview the anchor drove me back to my house in his car, but as we pulled onto my street I saw giant news trucks and groups of reporters surrounding my house. I felt scared and overwhelmed. We turned around and the news anchor took me to get something to eat, and then I went back to the hotel where I did the interview and I stayed by myself in the room overnight. I locked the door and I turned on the TV and I watched a news report about the standoff. I flipped channels and watched another report. I saw a photo of me flash on the screen. None of it made any sense. They might as well have been talking about another person and another incident.

I checked my phone and there were a million messages on it. Basically it had not stopped vibrating since around the middle of the standoff. I switched it off and got in bed and just lay there for a while in silence.

How weird, I thought as I lay there. *How weird.*

And then another thought made me sit bolt upright in bed.

My children!

I called Derrick first. He was hanging out with a friend that day, and I was afraid he'd heard about the shooting and didn't know if I was safe. It turns out someone did mention the incident to him, but all they said was, "There's a shooting in some Georgia school." There are thousands of schools in Georgia, and he had no way of knowing it was at McNair. I reached him on the phone and told him what happened, and told him I was fine.

"Mommy, are you okay?" he kept asking over and over. "Are you sure you're okay?"

"Yes, baby, I'm okay," I told my boy.

Later, he and I talked about the incident. "At first I was really angry at the idiot who held a gun to my momma's head," Derrick told me. "But when I heard the guy had mental issues, I could see how you were able to do what you did. I knew you were prepared for that. It's what you've always done."

> ANOTHER THOUGHT MADE ME SIT BOLT UPRIGHT IN BED. *MY CHILDREN!*

My next call was to LaVita. She found out about the shooting that afternoon, but knew little more for the next few hours until I was able to send her a text letting her know I was okay.

From the hotel room, I could finally fill her in on everything that happened.

As the last minutes of August 20 ticked away, I got up to make sure the hotel room door was locked, shut off my phone, turned off the TV, and got under the crisp white bed sheets. I closed my eyes and I had my quiet time. I tried to push everything else out of my brain—the fragments of memory and dialogue, the scary sight of the SWAT team approaching, the sound of Michael asking softly, "Do you remember me?"—and focus only on talking to God.

"Thank you, Father, for one more day," I prayed. "Thank You for this victory."

Sometime around midnight I drifted off to sleep. But it was a restless, fitful sleep. Much as I tried, I couldn't get my brain to shut down. People and places and events swirled around in there nonstop. The past and the present, and maybe even the future, unspooled in there like little movies. I envisioned Apostle Tuff, teaching me how to anchor myself in God—teaching me to be steadfast and unmovable. I saw my friend from the church—the one who helped save me on New Year's Eve. I thought of my ex-husband, and I tried to imagine what he thought when he heard about the standoff. Was he worried for my safety? Did he care enough to call to see if I was okay?

As I lay in bed I saw my children, both when they were young and as they are now. And I saw Derrick stretched out in the back of that rental car, uncomfortable and in pain, the two of us singing along to gospel songs, believing God would guide us home and give us life, not death. I saw my grandmother from way back when, picking wild flowers with me and teaching me not to be afraid of rattlesnakes. "You don't let them scare you," she taught me. "You scare them."

The image of Michael Hill was also there, in my mind, as I tried to slip into sleep. I saw his angry, contorted face, and the blood streaming down his arm. I saw him lay himself gently on the floor. I saw him jumped on and handcuffed and rushed away to his punishment. When I thought of Michael that night, I didn't feel any fear or anger. Hard as it may be to believe, all I felt was love.

In my foggy half-awake, half-asleep state, I heard Shirley Caesar still singing to me, still praising Him, though she had long since done her job and seen me through the darkness. I dreamed of the hole in the chain link fence and I imagined hundreds of frightened children filing through, each a tiny, perfect creation, each the center of someone's world, each beautiful in his or her own way. They would be asleep by now, safely tucked away in their beds, thoroughly kissed and hugged by their parents—hugged tighter and longer than most nights, for sure, until maybe even they pushed away because Mommy and Daddy were hugging them too hard.

Mostly, though, I let the words of a Bible verse play over and over in my mind, stream over me pure and clear like water over rocks—the very verse I began my day with, the very words I begin every day with.

> The Lord is my shepherd; I shall not want.
> He maketh me to lie down in green pastures:
> he leadeth me beside the still waters.
> He restoreth my soul: he leadeth me in the paths
> of righteousness for his name's sake.
> Yea, though I walk through the valley of the shadow of
>   death,
> I will fear no evil: for thou art with me;
> thy rod and thy staff they comfort me.
> Thous preparest a table before me in the presence of
>   mine enemies: thou anointest my head with oil; my
>   cup runneth over.
> Surely goodness and mercy shall follow me all the days
>   of my life:
> and I will dwell in the house of the Lord for ever.

And so did August 20 pass, by the grace of God.
The Devil laid no claim upon our souls that day.

///////////////////////////////////////

If any one purifies himself
from what is ignoble, then
he will be a vessel for noble
use, consecrated and useful
to the master of the house,
ready for any good work.

2 Timothy 2:21 RSV

///////////////////////////////////////

CHAPTER ELEVEN

It's very strange to wake up one morning and find yourself being called a hero. On TV, in newspapers, on websites, you see your own name next to a word usually reserved for soldiers and police officers and firefighters. "Antoinette Tuff Hailed as a Hero," read one headline a day or two after the standoff at McNair. "Real-Life Superhero Stops a Shooting," read another. "Hero School Clerk in Atlanta School Shooting Scare," someone else wrote. All these headlines are very, very humbling.

But they are also very, very wrong.

Hero is not the word I would use to describe myself on August 20. The word I would use is *vessel*.

As I've said before, the words that came out of my mouth, and the steadiness of my nerves, were not my work or my achievement—they were God's work and God's achievement.

The victory earned that day was not my victory—it was God's victory.

The one who was in control in that office was not me, or the shooter, or the police, or anyone else—the one who was in control was God.

All I did was serve as God's vessel.

There is nothing special about me that enabled me to be a vessel for God. The truth is, God uses us all to accomplish His work. He can turn any one of us into an instrument of good. What happened to me that day can happen to each and every one of us, at any moment, in any situation. We just never know when that moment is coming, or what that situation will be. But we are all capable of being God's vessel—of fulfilling the purpose God has chosen for us. "If any one purifies himself from what is ignoble, then he will be a vessel for noble use," the Bible tells us in 2 Timothy 2:21, "consecrated and useful to the master of the house, ready for any good work" (RSV).

The story of the standoff at McNair Academy is not a story about heroism. It is a story about being a vessel for God's noble use.

//////

I understand that the events of August 20 were unusual and unlikely, and that they play into a lot of hot-button issues in our society today, and that's why so many people around the world have been so interested in what happened at McNair. I also understand that, sadly, most incidents like the one at McNair do not end as peacefully as they did in our school. Like I said, Michael Hill came in talking, not shooting, and that gave everyone the opportunity to prevent a tragedy. But that opportunity is not always there. We have all lived through far too many shootings that end horrifically.

I was reminded of that just twenty-seven days after the standoff at McNair. Let me tell you that story.

Just two days after August 20, I was flown to New York City to appear on a national news show. My daughter, LaVita, came with me. We were staying in a hotel room waiting to do the taping when my cell phone rang. Now, so many people called me in the days after the incident that I basically handed my phone over to LaVita and had her deal with them. She's really good at handling things like that. So when my phone rang in the hotel room I didn't make any move to answer it. After a couple of rings LaVita said, "Mommy, answer your phone."

WE ARE ALL CAPABLE OF BEING GOD'S VESSEL—OF FULFILLING THE PURPOSE GOD HAS CHOSEN FOR US.

"No way," I said.

"Mommy, just answer it," LaVita repeated.

"Uh, uh," I said.

"Mommy, answer the phone!" LaVita yelled. "It's probably the president of the United States!"

It seems LaVita had already been in touch with someone who wanted to arrange a phone call between President Obama and me, and she hadn't told me about it because she wanted it to be a surprise.

I jumped to answer the phone.

"Hello?" I said.

"Ms. Antoinette Tuff?" a male voice asked.

"Yes, that's me."

"Ma'am, this is the White House calling."

I put my hand over the phone and turned to my daughter.

"Girl, it's the White House calling!"

"I know, Mommy, that's what I said!"

I went back to the phone call.

"You mean the real White House?" I asked.

"Yes ma'am, the real White House. President Obama's office."

The man was calling to coordinate the actual call from the president. Now here's the funny part: I told him I might not be able to take the call because I was due to tape the TV show.

Imagine that: me telling the president I'm busy.

We made plans to have the call sometime before the taping, and LaVita and I went over to the TV studio in Manhattan. I was sitting in a makeup chair when LaVita ran in with my cell phone.

"It's him!!" she squealed.

I took the phone. The same man was on the line, only this time he said, "Please hold for the president." Next thing I knew I was talking to President Obama.

"I just want to let you know that my family and I are very proud of you and what you did to save those children," he said. "We think you did a really good job."

I thanked him, and I think I told him he was doing a pretty good job himself. Then the president asked if I had been scared during the standoff, and I admitted I was, and I described some of what happened, and I told him I had to hide my emotions so the gunman wouldn't see them and get even more upset. We talked a little more, and to my surprise the president said he and his wife, Michelle, and their kids hoped to get the chance to meet me. I told him I hoped to meet him, too.

"Y'all have my number, so give me a call anytime," I said.

In fact, someone from the president's office did call me back a few days later and invited LaVita and me to the White House.

We were at the airport about to board a flight to the Washington DC area when we first heard there had been a shooting in DC that morning.

Over the course of that day, September 16, we got the details of what happened bit by bit. A civilian contractor walked into the Washington Navy Yard complex, just a little over two miles from the White House, and at 8:20 a.m. began shooting at employees with a shotgun. There was panic and chaos as people ran for their lives and the gunman kept shooting. "It was unbelievable how many shots were going off," one person said. After a long, running gun battle, tactical officers killed the shooter, but by then he had managed to kill twelve Navy Yard workers and injure several more. The crime scene was "one of the worst things we've seen in Washington," one police chief said.

> "MA'AM, THIS IS THE WHITE HOUSE CALLING."

Later it was discovered the shooter suffered from severe mental problems. He entered the scene dressed in black and carrying a black bag, like Michael Hill, and he stuffed his pants pockets full of bullets, also like Michael. But unlike Michael, the Navy Yard gunman did not come in talking. He came in shooting. There was no chance for anyone to try and stop him.

LaVita and I were in a car on our way to meet the president on September 16, when the full extent of the tragedy became clear.

Just forty minutes before the meeting, the White House called to say they'd canceled the event.

I was shocked when I heard about the shooting. It was an awful, horrifying reminder that most incidents involving mentally troubled shooters do not end peacefully. I said prayers for the victims and their loved ones, and for our whole country, that we might be strong in a time of such despair. The truth is we do not always understand how God works, and why things happen the way they do.

But even on that terrible day there was evidence of the power of compassion.

In the moments after the first shots were fired, workers scrambled to get out of the building as fast as possible. But one man, Omar Grant, didn't run out right away. Instead he went to find a co-worker who was visually impaired. He knew his co-worker would have a hard time making his way out of the building in such chaos. Omar found the man, took him by the arm, and walked him out of the building. By himself Omar would have made it to safety much, much faster. But he stayed with his co-worker until they were both out of harm's way.

You see, God uses us all to accomplish His work. He can turn any one of us into an instrument of good.

/////

Yet God doesn't just pick us randomly for whatever assignment He has for us. God does something else that is at the very heart of my story.

God gives us a purpose, and God *prepares* us for that purpose.

Just look at everything that happened in my life leading up to August 20, 2013.

For most of my life I was a caregiver—I spent hours every day taking care of my husband and taking care of my children. I never left my son Derrick's side as he struggled every day for years to do things most people take for granted. Like so many hardworking mothers and fathers and caregivers out there, I was up before the sun and still working when it went down, just about seven days a week. I did all of that very happily, and I considered it a blessing that I was able to take care of the people I loved. I'm just saying that, if I had to put a name on what it is I did with my life, I would say I was a caregiver.

And it wasn't just at home with my family. At work I was a caregiver, too. As a bookkeeper, I helped teachers and staffers handle their paperwork, and as a substitute teacher in the afterschool program, I helped students with their homework. As one of the leaders of the Cool Girl program, I helped female students with discipline and self-esteem issues start to believe in themselves and become leaders instead of followers. I took them on outings and tried to boost their confidence and taught them to be responsible for their own behavior. When I joined the program, we had about forty girls signed up to be Cool Girls, and most of them didn't take the program too seriously. Within a year, the Cool Girls were considered some of the brightest lights in the whole school, and we had parents begging us to let their daughters join. We had to start a waiting list that got longer every year.

And so every day, in some way, I found myself caring for someone. I tried to see the worthiness in those who struggled, tried to

God doesn't just pick us randomly for whatever assignment He has for us. . . . God gives us a purpose, and God prepares us for that purpose.

see the spark in those who dwelt in darkness. I tried to be strong for those who were weak, and I tried to hold up those who would fall. That was my life, month after month, year after year, for as long as I can remember. And I loved my life, until it all came crashing down in the months before August 20.

Yet there I was, filling in for the receptionist at McNair—though it easily could have been someone else—and trying to put on a brave face—though I had just gotten a phone call that ripped me apart. The whole, long journey of my life led me to that front office on that day and at that moment, and even though I believed I was too weak and powerless to take care of myself, much less anyone else, I was put there for a reason that God understood, even if I didn't.

Because just as my journey led me to that office and that front desk on that day, Michael Hill's long, difficult journey led him to the very same place. And when, more than anything else, he needed someone to listen to him, the person there to listen to him was me. And though he spoke with hatred, I listened with love. And though he struggled, I saw his worth. And though he dwelt in darkness, I searched for his spark. And because he was weak, I was strong, and because he would fall, I held him up. Those were the things I did every day. Those were the things I was *prepared* to do.

I did not have to pretend to be someone or say things I didn't believe: The person I was with Michael is the person I am—the person God prepared me to be.

But my life as a caregiver was not the only thing that prepared me for that fateful day. The reason I was able to show Michael Hill compassion, and feel the depths of his pain, and find it in my heart to love him, is because, in a way, I *was* Michael Hill. I understood the torment of having no place to go and no one to turn to, because I felt those very things myself. I understood the utter hopelessness that makes you believe you have no choice but to do something terrible, because in my darkest hours I felt that very same hopelessness. Like Michael, I stood at the brink of disaster, convinced that was the only way to escape my unbearable pain.

> I WAS PUT THERE FOR A REASON THAT GOD UNDERSTOOD, EVEN IF I DIDN'T.

Like Michael, I told myself I was ready to die.

But when I stood at the brink, God pulled me back, and because He did, I was at McNair Academy the day Michael Hill needed someone to pull him back.

And I understood that it was only by God's grace and mercy that I survived, so when I told Michael, "Baby, it's going to be all right," I was not just trying to placate him, I was telling him *what I knew to be true.* All the pain I felt, all the tears I cried, all the moments I felt worthless—that was all preparation for my assignment from God! That was God preparing me to be His instrument of good!

And here is the great beauty of God's system of preparation and purpose—all it takes for us to be prepared is to empty ourselves of ignoble things so we can be His vessel. "Do nothing from selfishness or conceit," it says in Philippians 2:3–4, "but in humility count others better than yourselves. Let each of you look not only to his own interests, but also to the interests of others" (RSV).

Humility, compassion, selflessness—yes, live a life filled with those things and we will be prepared for our purpose. Admit we are weak and flawed and no better than any other, and we will be prepared for our purpose. Recognize God is the source of our strength, and that apart from Him we can do nothing, as it says in John 15:5, and we will be prepared for our purpose. Ask ourselves, every morning when we get up, "Lord, how will You use me today? How can I be your instrument of good?" and we will be prepared for our purpose.

Open our hearts to the possibility God will call on us one day and ask us to be an angel for someone, and realize God puts people in our paths to guide us on our whirlwind journeys, and await our next assignment from God with thanks and praise and joyfulness, and we will be prepared for our purpose.

And when we are prepared, there is only one question we need to ask—the very question I asked in that office when Michael Hill walked in:

"God, what are we going to do now?"

Afterword

The events of August 20 changed my life, but they didn't change everything in my life. I still had a lot of the same problems, the same challenges. For instance, I still had to deal with my canceled bankruptcy repayment plan and find a way to keep my house and my car and my furniture. I remember calling Terry about it from the airport as I was on my way to New York City to appear on a TV show. But that call, like so many others, knocked me down. "You're the celebrity," I recall him telling me. "You pay the bills." It was another reminder that the thirty-three years we spent together meant nothing to him anymore. I sat in the airport and cried for a long time because I was still weak and still in pain, and I still missed my husband. I was still terrified of being alone.

The only difference this time, though, was that I knew everything was going to be okay. I knew God would lead me to still waters.

And anyway, I have so many blessings in my life, lately too many to count. After the incident at McNair I got hundreds of notes and letters and presents from people all over the world, thanking me for what I'd done. People sent me sweaters and scarves and stuffed animals and plaques and poems and so many beautiful things. One school in another state got all their children together and had them sign a giant purple banner, and they sent it to me and now it's up on a wall in my house. One day when I was praying to God because I couldn't pay an important bill, I opened my mail and found a certified check from a complete stranger in the *exact* amount of the bill I owed. Coincidence? Like I said, I don't believe in coincidences when God is involved.

> I HAVE SO MANY BLESSINGS IN MY LIFE, LATELY TOO MANY TO COUNT.

I also got to meet some incredible people, including Kendra McCray, the DeKalb County 9-1-1 dispatcher who was on the phone with me for much of the standoff at McNair, and whose composure and bravery played a big part in the outcome. Kendra is a lovely young woman, and it is an honor to know her. And guess what? I got to meet the president after all. A congressman invited LaVita and me to be his guests at an event on Capitol Hill, and we found ourselves in a line with people waiting to visit with the president and his wife. There were a lot of people in that line, and we waited a lot longer than I expected to wait, and wouldn't you know it, I had to go to the bathroom really badly again. I even snuck away and made a run for the restroom, until a Secret Service agent stopped me and said I was breaching security.

"If you go," he said, "you can't come back in."

So like I did at the school, I held my mule and tried not to think about it when we met the president and his wife, who hugged us and told us how proud they were. I remember Michelle pulling LaVita

222

aside and congratulating her for studying to become a lawyer. In fact, Michelle studied the same kind of law LaVita was studying. I listened to their conversation and thought about how truly blessed I was. My daughter, talking to the president's wife. Lord, how far we'd come.

Which brings me to the greatest blessings in my life—my beautiful children. LaVita, so smart and so feisty, became only the second woman on my mother's side to ever graduate college, and the very first to earn a graduate degree. And soon she will become the first to graduate from law school. Three degrees—that's pretty good. I wanted her to be a curse breaker, and she is.

So is my remarkable son, Derrick. He became the very first man among all my mother's ancestors to attend college. Despite his many challenges, he has refused to see himself as disabled in any way, and he lives his life with a joyous spirit that makes my heart swell. Sometimes, when I look at my son, I wonder if God has some special covenant with the damaged and the infirmed. Does He bestow some special grace on those who face the toughest struggles?

When I was at my very worst, when I thought I was all out of options, it was Derrick who called me into his room, sat down next to me and hugged me, and sang me a sweet gospel song he'd just written for me.

It is called "This Is My Season."

> I am claiming it now, this is my season
> I am claiming it now, this is my day
> Jesus, I know the storm is over
> So let Your blessings fill this place

I am claiming it now, that I will conquer
Everything that comes my way
Because by Your Word I am victorious
There is nothing greater than Your name

How was my son able to speak God's words to me when I couldn't hear them myself? How could he have been the strong one who saved me, and not the other way around? Maybe he has some special covenant with God after all.

I am so very blessed in so many different ways, but in the end—though I have spent all this time talking about my life—my story only matters if there is something *you* can take away from it. If there is something in it to make your life more meaningful and bring you closer to God. I pray God's message of preparation and purpose shines through the words in this book. And I pray we allow God to use us as His vessels, so that we may put our faith to work and show it through good deeds.

/////

I have not spoken to Michael Hill since August 20. He was charged with aggravated assault and terroristic threats, and he will go through the judicial system. He shot at police officers and he terrorized hundreds of people, and he will be punished for that. Many nights I pray for Michael, pray he gets the help he needs. There were many people who did show great compassion to Michael Hill along the way, and who did try and give him the help he needed, but somehow he slipped through the cracks. I pray that others in his position don't ever feel so hopeless and out of options.

For weeks after August 20, I had trouble sleeping. I had terrible nightmares, some of which had Michael Hill in them, some that had my ex-husband. Some of the nightmares were about being alone for the first time in my life. For weeks after the incident, I'd wake up in terror. But over time the nightmares lessened and the terror subsided. Maybe an event like the standoff leaves an imprint on your brain that takes a long time to fade away, if it ever does. But that's okay—I'm doing just fine. I have my kids. I have my quiet time. I have God.

> MY STORY ONLY MATTERS IF THERE IS SOMETHING YOU CAN TAKE AWAY FROM IT.

Not long ago I went on an outing to the mall with my Cool Girls from McNair. We watched a movie and had a bite to eat, and then we went to one of those stores where you can create your own stuffed teddy bear. All the girls made their own bears and put them in silly outfits and gave them names. I made a bear, too, and when one of the Cool Girls asked me what my bear's name was, I had to think about it for a minute.

All of a sudden a name popped in my head.

"My bear's name is New Beginning," I said.

"New Beginning?" the girl asked.

"Yes," I said. "New Beginning."

After all, that is the gift that God gave me.

For Personal Reflection or Book Club Discussion

1. August 20 starts like any normal day for Antoinette. What does the way she starts her day say about her? What does the way you start your day say about you?

2. As a child, Antoinette was treated the way no child should be treated. How do you think this helped shaped her into the woman she became on August 20? How have specific events from your childhood helped—or hindered—you?

3. Even from an early age, Antoinette never shied away from being herself—even when it got her into trouble. And it was her, being herself, that changed the course of events on August 20. When was a time that being true to yourself solved a problem or eased a situation for you?

4. After reading the inside account of the events on August 20, has your view of Michael Hill, the gunman, changed? Why or why not?

5. Antoinette's son, Derrick, was a constant encouragement to her—and bright light in her story. Who is this in you life? What have you learned from him or her?

6. Every morning, Antoinette would anchor herself in hope and faith by talking, and listening, to God. How do you anchor yourself in life? If you don't, what are ways you could start doing this?

7. In an unthinkable situation, Antoinette was able to genuinely love a hurting—and many would say unlovable—young man back from the brink. Is there a time in your life when love triumphed over the bad?

8. There has been a lot of heartbreak, abandonment, and betrayal in Antoinette's life. When was a time you felt betrayed or abandoned? How did you react? How did you recover?

9. What do you see as the turning point for the events on August 20? Why?

10. Antoinette's life has changed completely since August 20. What has been a watershed moment in your life? Have things changed for the better or worse since then? Why?

11. Looking back through her story, it's clear Antoinette was prepared for a purpose. If you look back on your life, what

have you been prepared for? Are you still in the midst of that preparation?

12. Where do you see yourself in Antoinette's story? What parts of her story can you relate to the most?

//

THEREFORE, IF ANY ONE IS IN
CHRIST, HE IS A NEW CREATION;
THE OLD HAS PASSED AWAY,
BEHOLD, THE NEW HAS COME.

2 Corinthians 5:17 RSV

//

ACKNOWLEDGMENTS

First and foremost, thank You to God. On August 20, 2013, You set me on a new journey, and my destiny changed from the one I thought I had to the one You chose for me.

Thank you, also, to all the angels God sent me at every step of the way, so that even though I went to hell and back, I never gave in to what Satan had in mind for me. God turns curses into blessings, and because of these angels I stayed in God's good grace and mercy, and for that I can't thank you all enough: my son Derrick Tuff, Apostle Ulysses Tuff, Brenda Roseboro, John Roseboro, my aunt Jean Milan, my uncle Tony Milan, my aunt Charlie Mae Tuff-Barber, Juanita Vaughn, Anthony Dockery, Gayle Davis, Dr. Keshier Smikle, Kia Dennis, John Wilson (Mr. Hickey), Dr. Ruben A. Alexander, Charles Barnes, Vanessa Johnson, and Melvin Copland.

Thanks also to Tim Peterson, Carra Carr, Jeff Braun, and everyone at Bethany House for helping me tell my story, to Alex Tresniowski for his writing talent, and to Hatti Hill, Jan Miller, Nena Madonia, and everyone at Dupree/Miller for believing in me.

A special thanks to all my new friends who continue to send me cards, notes, poems, gifts, awards, honors, prayers, and love. May God open up the windows of heaven and pour out so many blessings on you all that you don't even have enough room for them.

Antoinette Tuff is a true picture of grace, courage, leadership, and heroism at its best. But before she made headlines and talked a school shooter back from the brink, she was a woman who faced—and overcame—her own pain and hurt. Publicly recognized by President Obama for her courageous act that saved a school from tragedy, today she speaks around the world, spreading hope and sharing her inspiring message of how our lives prepare us for our own moments of purpose. She has two children and resides in Atlanta, Georgia.

Alex Tresniowski is a former PEOPLE Magazine senior writer and the author of eleven books, including recent bestsellers *An Invisible Thread* and *Waking Up in Heaven*. Alex lives and works in New York City.